# Praise for
# *WHAT YOUR Clutter IS TRYING TO TELL YOU*

"Still beating yourself up about the jam-packed garage, the boxes still in the basement, or the overflowing closets and cabinets? Well, it's time to stop and read this book. *What Your Clutter Is Trying to Tell You* is not your typical 'clear your clutter and be happy' story. It spills the beans on why you haven't been motivated to handle the mess, and it shows you how to use your clutter as a catalyst for growth so you can create more space, prosperity, and peace in your life. Clutter isn't your enemy, it's your ticket to freedom, and Kerri Richardson will show you how!"

— **Cheryl Richardson**, *New York Times* best-selling author of
*The Art of Extreme Self-Care*

"Clutter is modern-day alchemy! In Kerri's gem of a book, she explains step-by-step the value of clearing out what isn't needed in your life, as well as some time-honored ways to do it. This book is instantly accessible. Anyone's life will improve by following the simple, yet profound, steps available in *What Your Clutter Is Trying to Tell You.* Highly recommended!"

— **Denise Linn**, best-selling author of *Sacred Space* and
*Feng Shui for the Soul*

"Kerri Richardson helps you clear the clutter in your life by figuring out why it's in your life to begin with. It not only helps you eliminate physical clutter, but emotional and mental blockages too, creating space for your soul to be energized! This is a must-read for everyone!"

— **John Holland**, psychic medium, spiritual teacher,
and best-selling author of *Born Knowing*

"I absolutely love Kerri Richardson's no-nonsense, practical, and action-oriented approach to clearing space and cultivating energy by first putting attention on the obstacles blocking our abundance. *What Your Clutter Is Trying to Tell* is an easy-to-follow guide that will support you in finally clearing the clutter that collects in countless ways, leaving you unencumbered on your path to liberation and abundance."

— **Nancy Levin**, author of *Worthy*

"Kerri Richardson brilliantly bridges the gap between physical clutter and the flow of energy in our lives. With quick, easy, and approachable exercises, one begins to understand that our soul truly needs clarity to live the fullest life. *What Your Clutter Is Trying to Tell You* is a gentle reminder to be conscious of choices and mindful of our surroundings."

— **Dougall Fraser**, author of *Your Life in Color*

# WHAT YOUR *Clutter* IS TRYING TO TELL YOU

## UNCOVER THE MESSAGE IN THE MESS AND RECLAIM YOUR LIFE

### KERRI L. RICHARDSON

**HAY HOUSE, INC.**
Carlsbad, California • New York City
London • Sydney • Johannesburg
Vancouver • New Delhi

*Published and distributed in the United States by:* Hay House, Inc.: www.hayhouse.com® • *Published and distributed in Australia by:* Hay House Australia Pty. Ltd.: www.hayhouse.com.au • *Published and distributed in the United Kingdom by:* Hay House UK, Ltd.: www.hayhouse.co.uk • *Published and distributed in the Republic of South Africa by:* Hay House SA (Pty), Ltd.: www.hayhouse.co.za • *Distributed in Canada by:* Raincoast Books: www.raincoast.com • *Published in India by:* Hay House Publishers India: www.hayhouse.co.in

*Cover design:* Scott Breidenthal • *Interior design:* Bryn Starr Best
*Interior illustrations:* Shutterstock.com

Library of Congress Cataloging-in-Publication Data on file

**Tradepaper ISBN:** 978-1-4019-5301-0

10  9  8  7  6  5  4  3  2
1st edition, August 2017

Printed in the United States of America

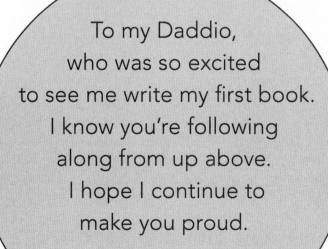

To my Daddio,
who was so excited
to see me write my first book.
I know you're following
along from up above.
I hope I continue to
make you proud.

Love,
Bo7

# Contents

# Introduction

Over the past couple of years, I've downsized like a champ. I've gone from 2,000 square feet to 700 square feet to 500 square feet, all the while planning to live in a 230-square-foot tiny house (yes, like the ones you see on those TV shows). I've done the sorting and purging. I've faced the difficult decisions. I've processed the guilt from giving away gifts and heirlooms. I've set challenging boundaries. I've said good-bye to draining friendships. And I've worked hard to excavate the stories in the stuff to understand what my clutter was trying to tell me. Doing so has not only helped me create space in my life, but also allowed me to learn about myself in ways I never had before.

I've never been a pack rat, but I've been known to get my fix from retail therapy now and then. And I've fallen victim to the idea of "have space, must fill."

This latter trait became especially apparent back when my wife, Melissa, and I made the move from a small apartment to a 2,000-square-foot house. My in-laws had come over to help us set up and make the place feel like home. My father-in-law, a genius at decorating, puts together magazine-worthy rooms.

"Before you go to bed," he said, "leave out all of your home-decor items. I'll be awake before you, so I'll get going on decorating."

Great! We were excited to see what magic he would work.

When we woke up the next morning, one room was beautifully set up. The others? Barren.

"Where's the rest of your stuff?" he asked. "I used everything you had in that one room."

Well, we had come from a small apartment.

"That was everything," I said, as I shrugged.

"Guess we'd better go shopping," he said.

And so it began. We had rooms to fill, walls to adorn, and windows to dress. With it being just the two of us, we certainly didn't need a house with a living room and a family room, an eat-in kitchen and a dining room, or three bedrooms and two full bathrooms. But that's what the world tells us success is: more and bigger.

After a handful of years living in the house, I began to tire of the upkeep. A full cleaning took hours. Yard work was eating up weekends. This was not how we wanted to spend our time. Deep down I knew this white-picket-fence lifestyle wasn't for me, but I had gotten caught up in "keeping up with the Joneses."

For some, a large house or many belongings may truly bring joy, but I realized in these moments that that's just one template for life. I had long subscribed to the belief that it was the only template. I loved my house and neighborhood, but felt my property and its contents owned me instead of me owning them. Many of the items no longer brought me joy. Often, I felt weighed down by my stuff instead of uplifted by it. That's when I knew I was surrounded by clutter: physical, financial, and emotional. If this was success, I wasn't interested.

One day, for shits and giggles, I said to Melissa, "Do you ever think about cashing it all in and taking off?"

"You mean, sell the house?" she asked.

My question had been rhetorical, but I figured I'd play along. "I hadn't thought that far, but sure, yeah, sell the house."

"I have thought of it," she said. "You know, we could move to a different country. Belize is nice and warm. They speak English. They use U.S. currency, and there's a huge expat community. And it's not too far, so if we needed to come home, the travel would be easy."

Whoa, whoa, whoa. She had clearly given this some serious thought.

"Okay," I said, "that might be a little extreme. Maybe we start by traveling the United States in an RV for a couple of years."

While I was surprised by how much thought she'd given this, I was relieved and excited to hear she'd be open to change too. I wasn't the only one feeling burdened by the house and all the stuff and responsibilities that came with it.

After a lot of research, soul-searching, and discussions, we decided to build a tiny house on wheels instead. I love the idea of "form follows function" and that we'd get to design our space to perfectly suit our specific, unique needs. Instead of buying a house and figuring out how to use the rooms, we would look at our priorities and how we use space and build accordingly. You have to consider how you'll use every inch when you'll be living in a 230-square-foot house!

It was time to simplify, and simplify we did. Clearly the universe was behind us, because as we were selling things online, I stumbled upon a post in a Facebook yard sale group. Someone asked if anyone in our town was planning on listing their house soon. What are the chances of someone looking for a property at a virtual yard sale site? Usually you find a bookcase or a lamp in there, but a house? I figured it couldn't hurt to message the poster, so I did. Two weeks later, we had a generous offer. One month later, we closed. Thanks, Uni! (The universe and I are tight, so I gave it a nickname.)

Moving is a real pain in the ass, but it's also a great chance to clear out. And with plans to go from a house to a tiny house, we had some serious downsizing to do.

We created a simple moving sale website and used virtual yard sale sites to sell some items, donated quite a bit, and gave some furniture and decor to family and friends. We ended up making about $5,000 in sales, plus having a whole bunch of tax write-offs. Most importantly, however, was that we reclaimed our freedom, energy, and power.

This is not to say it was easy. There were many times when I struggled to part with an item. Maybe it had been a gift, or something I really loved at one time and had a hard time accepting that I no longer did. Or if something had cost a decent amount of money, I felt like I should hang on to it.

To keep my eye on the prize, I'd remind myself why I was doing this at all: to live a life aligned with my personal valuation of experiences over things and to no longer adhere to the traditional definition of success. I liked having nice things, but for me, that joy was temporary, whereas the memory of a cool experience or fun adventure would stay with me forever.

As I sorted through items, I asked myself some questions to gain clarity. Things like:

- Does this item represent who I am now?

- If I saw this in a store today, would I buy it?

- What feelings are triggered by this item? Guilt? Dread? Excitement?

- Do I use or display this item?

Doing this helped me decide if the item *deserved* to stay in my life. I had only so much space and energy available, and I no longer wanted to spend them frivolously.

Sure, my situation may seem extreme, but it allowed me to see what I truly needed to be happy and what I truly loved and wanted in my life.

I was surprised by how little that translated to.

As a lifestyle designer and coach, I've helped thousands of people see what's stopping them from making a change, and it's often not what they think. Clutter clogs up more than floors, tables, and closets. It blocks abundance. It suffocates dreams. It dims your light.

While physical clutter can be overwhelming and exhausting, it holds insights and answers to some of your biggest blocks. By digging into your clutter and unearthing what it's trying to tell you, you can understand the message in the mess and see the limitless possibilities and new opportunities that are yours for the taking.

As you work through the exercises in this book, you'll see that any dread you feel is a powerful indicator of a root issue. You'll also understand your clutter in a way that allows you to feel compassion and curiosity toward it instead of loathing and fear.

While I offer sorting and organizing tips in every chapter, *What Your Clutter Is Trying to Tell You* is really about discovering all the wonderful facets of yourself by using clutter as a clue. Will you clear clutter as a result? Absolutely. But this is more about excavating your energetic blocks so you can get to the business of living a kick-ass life.

We're digging deep here. Clutter is a beautiful tool for self-exploration, self-understanding, and self-compassion. To sink your teeth into this concept, you'll have to act. The learning comes with the doing. Go through the exercises, maybe even more than once. It's time for you to reclaim your life. And you might even make some money in the process!

## Chapter 1

# Clutter: Monster or Messenger

**Clutter.** Even the word feels heavy when you say it. We've become consumed by stuff and so inundated by things that we almost have nowhere to turn. In the United States alone, there are more than 2.63 billion square feet of self-storage space. That's more than three times the size of the island of Manhattan! And the occupancy rate of these facilities is 90 percent.

Nearly 1 in 10 U.S. households rents a storage unit, even though 65 percent of those households have a garage.[1] That's not surprising, because the average U.S. household contains 300,000 things![2] While the United States leads the pack in the amount of storage space rented, Canada and Australia are big fans too.

As we buy more and more, our homes, garages, attics, cars, and lives are bursting at the seams.

We think the problem is
not having enough space for our stuff, when in fact
it's that we have too much stuff for our space.

Clutter is a roadblock to abundance in all its forms. Whether it's physical clutter that is frustrating you or emotional clutter that limits your thinking, if you don't have space in your life and mind, the universe can't send you the goods. If you want a different job, a better relationship, more money, or loving friends, but your life is filled with toxic relationships, boxes of mementos, or stacks and stacks of books, then you're literally clogging the path. Your space is telling a different story, and your words aren't matching your actions.

My client Susan came to me because she was struggling to get a new business off the ground and couldn't figure out what was getting in her way. After several conversations and a bit of digging, I learned she had storage bins containing remnants of a past unsuccessful venture under her bed. All that time, she had been sleeping above her failed business, which was not very inspiring for launching something new!

As she worked on emptying those bins, she got clear on where she wanted to take her new business, and it was in a completely different direction than she had originally thought. Clearing the bins didn't magically make her new business a raging success. Instead, it freed up her energy so she could clarify her focus. She then felt more able to make steady progress, and she reclaimed her belief in herself. And now that she wasn't sleeping above objects that represented failure to her, she also fell asleep easier and slept more soundly through the night.

When the clutter of negative thoughts, blocking beliefs, and piles of stuff surround you, it's nearly impossible to see better options or creative solutions to overcoming life's obstacles. Even the smallest amount of physical clutter can cause an energetic hoarding situation. The channels through which you and the universe communicate become narrower and narrower, making it difficult for things to ever feel like they're going your way. Open those channels by handling even a little bit of clutter, and you'll find yourself in the flow.

It's in that flow that gifts and opportunities are delivered. The universe and your spiritual team are always at the ready to support you, but they need to be invited in. Opening space in your life sends that invitation.

Clutter is not out to sabotage you. It's out to get your attention. It wants to show you where you're tripping yourself up or running in circles so you can work on the real obstacle instead of wasting time on the stuff.

When you look at clutter this way, you'll be able to be more understanding of and compassionate toward yourself for having the clutter to begin with.

Look at what benefit you get from keeping your clutter, and get into a relationship with your stuff instead of fighting it. Yes, I want you to become besties with your clutter. By doing so, you'll begin to see it as a messenger instead of a monster, which will allow you to understand it in a way that makes it easier to say good-bye to it once and for all.

I define *clutter* as anything that gets in the way of living the life of your dreams. This can be an outdated wardrobe that's overtaken your closet. It can be piles of paperwork that need your attention or that you don't know what to do with. It can also be your nagging inner critic, toxic relationships, debt, or extra body weight. Those friends who drain your energy? Clutter. Your belief that if you can't do it perfectly, then you shouldn't do it at all? Clutter.

**Clutter is a temper tantrum of the soul, and it's time to listen closely to what it's saying.**

Think of some things—or that one big thing—you'd love to do. I'll bet the next things that come to mind are all the reasons you can't possibly do those things: lack of time, a tight budget, too many commitments, or no related skills. All of that? Clutter.

Clearing clutter is about getting rid of anything that is no longer a fit for your life. It is about creating space for true fulfillment and joy and welcoming in the universal abundance that is waiting for you.

Some of your clutter has accumulated because of ineffective systems, but it all has an emotional component. When you explore what that component is, you reveal incredible insights into why you aren't accomplishing your goals and how you're getting in your own way over and over again.

Maybe you'd like to be in a loving romantic relationship, but you can't seem to find someone who fits the bill. What are your current relationships with friends and family like? Could they use some boundaries? If so, those dynamics are likely clogging up your relationship center and leaving no room for someone new.

Are you holding on to things from past relationships that cause you grief? That could be getting in the way.

Do you feel undeserving of love? This blocking belief might be the culprit.

That's all clutter.

Do you stress about money? Clutter in the form of blocking beliefs around money, a disorganized bill-paying system, or resentment of those who have more than you could very well be keeping the money away.

Clutter has a lot to tell you about what's off-balance in your life. It's like a flashing arrow pointing to the areas that need attention. Identify an aspect of your life that isn't going the way you'd like, and there will be corresponding clutter.

Realizing that there's a lot more clutter in your life than just physical items may seem like it complicates matters, but in fact it simplifies things. When you recognize that your clutter holds some life-changing clues, dealing with it becomes a treasure hunt. Rather than resisting the piles (physical and emotional) and hoping they'll magically go away, you can think about what those piles might be trying to tell you.

As we dive deep into the message in the mess, here are some questions to think about:

- What stops you from clearing your clutter? (Go beyond "I don't have time.")

- What would it mean if it was all gone? (Move past "I'd be relieved.")

- If clutter were no longer an obstacle, what would you then have time for? (This might be a professional pursuit, a romantic relationship, or a life dream.)

- Is there anything about that task, project, or goal that feels intimidating? (Might your clutter be a convenient distraction from pursuing that scary goal?)

You can't change what you aren't aware of. Your soul is trying desperately to get your attention. It has something to say and isn't feeling heard. The message might be a call to action or a cry for help. Either way, stubborn clutter is an indicator of a non-clutter issue.

My client Mike had a stubborn pile of paperwork stacked up on his kitchen table. In it were documents he needed to complete or file from his previous graphic design contract job—something he felt he had to do before he could find a new job. He would sort some of the pile, tossing, recycling, or filing certain items, but he'd always leave most of the documents there.

He said dealing with them would take too much time and that he needed a good three-hour block to get through them all. It's this kind of black-and-white thinking that was keeping him stuck. I challenged him to work on the pile in 15-minute chunks.

**With all-or-nothing thinking, nothing always wins.**

He would make some progress, but then the pile would grow again. After this happened a few times, I decided to take a different approach and asked Mike how he felt about finding a new job.

"It's something I have to do," he said. "I've enjoyed my time off, but the bills aren't going to pay themselves."

"Do you still like the type of contract work you're doing?"

"It's okay. It's not as creative as I'd like, but it pays the bills."

That was twice that Mike had mentioned work as a means to simply "pay the bills." I asked him to imagine doing creatively fulfilling work and to describe what that work would look like.

"Oh, man," he said, "I'd get to use my artistic eye and create something original for my clients. They'd look to me for input on the creation. In my old work, I felt like a monkey at the machine, just checking off the tasks on a list—not very inspiring. If I could be part of the creative process and the execution, that'd be sweet!"

"I can totally hear the difference in your voice," I said. "You sound plugged into the work now, and excited by the idea of doing it. If you could find that kind of work but still needed to handle that stack of papers first, how would you feel about clearing the pile?"

"Well, now I'm annoyed that those papers are stopping me."

Now we were getting somewhere. It wasn't a lack of time that kept the pile there. It was the fact that clearing it meant Mike would have to go back to an uninspiring job.

"What if the first step in getting rid of that pile is looking for this kind of cool, creative work instead of the other way around?"

"Sounds good to me!"

Off he went to look for inspiring work, and once he found some leads, the clutter pile became a nonissue. In fact, the documents that needed to be filed, tossed, or shredded took him just one hour instead of the three he had anticipated.

Soon he landed two contracts doing work he was excited about.

Mike had thought he had a clutter problem when in fact the stack of papers was simply a stalling tactic to avoid work he no longer enjoyed. While it might not have been something he was doing consciously, there was a part of him that knew exactly how to avoid the job hunt.

Seeing the papers every day was annoying, but what was bugging him more was the undone task taunting him: facing the fact that he hated the work he was doing and feeling trapped by bills. It wasn't about the paper clutter at all.

The whole world is an energetic exchange. In fact, all it takes is a shift in perspective to help you see other options and feel hopeful and motivated. When clutter is clogging your home and mind, it's as if you throw up a roadblock, making the flow of energy almost impossible.

You know those times when nothing seems to go right, when everything feels like a chore and you can't seem to catch a break?

Now think about when you feel totally in the flow. Everything is clicking and opportunities seem to just fall into your lap. That's the power of a clutter-free road. The energy can fly down the fast lane. And that, my friend, is what we want—for the lane to be clear, open, and newly paved so you can get and stay in the flow.

## *Action Time!*

Grab a journal or notebook or open a document on your computer and answer the following questions:

1. What have I dreamed about doing but haven't taken any or enough action on?

2. What is stopping me from giving that dream more time or attention?

3. What kinds of clutter showed up in my answer to question 2? (Remember, anything that stands in your way is clutter, so think about options for clearing whatever it is.)

When answering, let the words flow, pouring out whatever comes to mind. No censoring, no editing, no judging.

## Chapter 2

# The Secret behind Your Resistance

Doesn't the idea of open, flowing channels of abundance sound fantastic? To be free of the weight of *should*, fears, and overwhelming thoughts? Imagine that open space, allowing you to see options, opportunities, and possibilities. Pretty cool, right?

Even with that vision, you may feel completely unmotivated to do anything about clearing your clutter. So what's going on with the resistance? Are you lazy? A slob? Only you can say for sure, but even if you are one of those things (which I doubt), I can tell you there's more to it.

I'd like to introduce someone I'm sure you're quite familiar with: *your inner critic*. She's not a fan of change and will fight it at every turn. She's happy right where she is, where it's familiar and safe. She sees no reason to rock the boat. She is the puppet master behind your procrastination.

Even if it's clear the change you are striving for will make things better, your inner critic is not having it. She can be a real brat who wants things her way and her way only. Do something outside of her comfort zone, and she'll sound the warning bell to keep you right where you are.

And she's a clever one. She'll change the language of those sirens, grabbing whatever your most vulnerable thoughts are at the moment, to be sure to get your attention in the quickest and most effective way.

Let's say one fear is that the job will be too big to handle. She'll chatter on about things like:

"You'll never get that done. You need hours to tackle that. Maybe next weekend."

"Where will you even begin?"

"Maybe you should just hire a professional organizer."

Those distraction techniques have the greatest chance of stopping you in your tracks, because that's where your fear is currently focused.

Maybe you dread facing what's in those boxes. Your critic's script changes:

"You know you can't get rid of those cards. Mom gave them to you."

"Do you really want to be reminded of your failed marriage?"

"Oh, yeah, let's go through those books from the degree program you never finished."

And she's got you again.

But here's the thing: your inner critic is just a loving little liar. She really doesn't mean you any harm. She's scared, so she makes up all sorts of excuses so you won't make progress. Because in her eyes, any change is bad.

The clutter she thinks you can't handle could be what's stopping you from getting that dream job, finding that loving partner, traveling the world, or improving your health. It's not the clutter your inner critic wants to hold on to. Instead, it's the protection she believes it gives her from what seems to her like your big, scary goal.

**Your inner critic is a loving liar.**

My client Samantha talked about putting her house on the market for months. She and her boyfriend had been dating long distance for two years and had decided to move in together, with Samantha relocating to his area. She loved where her boyfriend lived, and she sounded excited to make it her home.

She knew she needed to clean out the garage before she could list her house—her real estate agent had made that clear. She had twice rallied friends and family to help get the space organized, and each time they had made some real progress, yet the space had filled up again.

"It feels like I take one step forward and two steps back," Samantha told me.

She and I talked about what kinds of things ended up back in the garage, making it cluttered again.

"Well, I let a friend put some boxes and lawn equipment in there, just for a few days, while he figures out what to do with it."

The "few days" turned into two weeks.

I shifted the conversation and asked her to tell me about her plans for relocating. How did she feel about it? Was she ready for this next step in the relationship? What was it like to think about no longer living where she currently did?

She started with the expected answers about how much she loved her boyfriend, how she was excited about this new chapter, how she was stressed about the logistics of moving.

And then she mentioned it—the key to the clutter. "I'm a little hesitant to be so far from my parents. They're healthy and independent, but they're no spring chickens."

As we talked more about her parents and her relationship with them, I learned she was the child who tended to take charge and organize when they needed something.

We spent the rest of our conversation brainstorming ideas on how she could still be intimately involved with their needs and care even from a distance. She talked to her siblings about her concern and asked for their help so they could all be more involved with their parents. Once Samantha had that conversation and got support from her siblings, she couldn't believe how much easier it became to clear out her garage.

Like Mike's stack of papers, it wasn't about the items in the garage. The part of her that feared change kept filling up the space to make her stay put. Her inner critic was sabotaging her progress not because she didn't want to move, but because there were unaddressed fears. When Samantha took the courageous step of asking her siblings for help, her critic felt supported and stepped aside as Samantha cleared the garage.

The combination of listening more deeply to what your soul is telling you and taking small steps to show there's nothing to be afraid of are keys to clearing the clutter that keeps you stuck. But when you let the resistance prevent you from taking action, you're telling your fear that it's right, that it is best to stay stuck. You hand your power over to it and continue running on the hamster wheel of your life, exerting a lot of energy and getting nowhere.

The best way to handle your critic, no matter how persistent or bratty she gets, is with love and compassion. When you join forces instead of fighting against her, there's no stopping you. You become a powerful team!

To best partner with your critic, you need to focus on well-defined steps. "Winging it" doesn't work for her. She is easily distracted, and therefore so are you. Eliminate as many distractions as possible and work within the parameters you set. To help her get comfortable with change, take things in super small steps. If you find yourself procrastinating, break down the action you're trying to do; chances are it's still too big for your critic. She needs evidence that she'll be safe to get on board, so don't expect her to take big leaps out of the gate.

The other thing she needs is to feel heard—hence the persistent squawking. This part is key. If ever she feels dismissed or ignored, chaos ensues. This chaos can take many shapes—more clutter, a nasty head cold that knocks you down for a week, a distracted mind, aches and pains, a family member or friend telling you not to get rid of this or that, or a sexy invitation for the exact time you had scheduled your clutter clearing—anything that will stop you in your tracks and throw a wrench in your clutter-clearing plans so she can continue on her merry way and not have her status quo disrupted.

When you do finally settle in to tackle your first bit of clutter from this perspective, you're likely going to feel a lot of pushback from her. Instead of ignoring it and diving in, take some time to acknowledge what's coming up as you consider starting the sorting or clearing. The first clutter you may need to clear is your resistance. Sit with it. Journal about it. Speak to someone safe. Give it a voice. This is what helps her settle down.

You may be the one doing the heavy lifting in the relationship, but that's not to say you're in charge all the time. You need each other. Your inner critic needs structure, commitment, and strategy, and you need her creativity, playfulness, and inquisitiveness, so when she's raising the red flags, take a moment to acknowledge her. Doing so will make you much more successful in your clearing.

In fact, I suggest you make it a regular part of your clutter-clearing routine. Each time you get ready to sort physical clutter or take steps to address emotional clutter, take a couple of minutes to check in with your resistance and see what's going on. Oftentimes, that check-in is all you need to remove the current block.

## *Action Time!*

Revisit an area of clutter that is giving you trouble. Bring along a notebook or journal. Set a timer for 10 minutes and answer this question: "What is it about this clutter that I find it so difficult to sort through?" Then let it flow. Just let whatever wants to come out come out.

When you're finished, take a few deep breaths to get centered, then read what you've just written. Read it with empathy. Read it with kindness and understanding. Let your inner critic know that you're right there with her.

After some loving reassurance, revisit the clutter and see if it feels any different.

. . . . . . . . . . . . . . . . . . . . . . . . . . . . . . . . . . . . . . . . . . . . .

## Chapter 3

# If Your Clutter Could Talk . . .

With your inner critic's resistance challenging you to keep your clutter right where it is, let's be sure you're considering all the creative ways it shows up in your life. When you think of clutter, you probably think of things like books, mail, files, toys, clothes, or kitchen accessories. You may not consider things like toxic relationships, inner-critic messages, regrets, grudges, and outdated thoughts. These different types of clutter affect one another, with one often causing the other.

After a long day at work, you come home to piles of stuff on your kitchen table, and your energy is sapped. You start beating yourself up for not taking care of it sooner. You get aggravated with family members who piled stuff there after you asked them not to. Suddenly, it's not just about the stuff on the table. The clutter becomes fodder for your inner critic to remind you how lazy you are, how your family doesn't respect you, and how your efforts are futile. Now imagine what that kind of thinking does to your hope of making positive changes in your life. Can you say *deflation*?

It works in reverse too. Neglect emotional clutter and you'll see how quickly it turns into physical clutter. For example, when you tolerate unhealthy relationships or agree to every request that comes your way, you become so drained that common household maintenance is neglected. Your outer world reflects your inner world; when there's internal unrest, it shows up in your environment.

My friend Brian was unhappy in his marriage and had been for quite a while. To numb his feelings, he turned to online shopping. Getting that box delivered gave him a bit of a high that helped him momentarily forget about his situation. He'd think about asking his wife for a divorce, but to be ready for that step, Brian felt he had to get rid of a bunch of stuff so he could easily move out after he spoke to her. But he would quickly get overwhelmed by the size of the job and put it off.

He found himself in a vicious cycle—wanting to leave his marriage, feeling like it'd be too much work, buying something else to numb out (resulting in having more stuff to get rid of), and finding himself back at the beginning.

Knowing that this wasn't working for him, he decided to take a different approach. In hope of lighting a fire under himself, he decided to ask for the divorce before getting rid of a single thing. You know what happened? His compulsive online shopping stopped. He began selling, donating, and gifting items easily, and he made quick progress on starting the next chapter of his life. Much to his surprise, the brave move of ending his marriage had needed to happen before he could detach emotionally from his clutter.

Brian's clutter was a symptom of his circumstance. Instead of handling the symptom, he handled it at the source.

To help you sink your teeth into this concept, let's explore the messages in some common clutter hot spots and in various types of specific clutter.

## COMMON CLUTTER HOT SPOTS

We all have areas where clutter tends to land, multiply, and live. These areas seem to be catchalls for either stuff we don't know what to do with or stuff that has outgrown its home. What hidden messages might these areas be holding? When you consider each hot spot in its entirety instead of the specific clutter within it, you can get the big-picture message your stuff is sending you.

### Closets

Closets are the places where we tuck away our dirty little secrets. Whether it's clothes in the back of your bedroom wardrobe that represent a happier or healthier time in your life or the junk-collecting closet that reflects old hobbies or goals, out of sight is never out of mind with clutter. Hidden clutter is an energy drain that is always calling for your attention, and it becomes fuel for your inner critic to squawk about what you *should* be doing.

### Counters/Tabletops

Clutter that you see often is a consistent energy vampire, but the solution isn't to tuck the items away in a drawer. The clutter that ends up on a tabletop is often the kind that an organizational system can handle effectively. For example, piles of mail can be eradicated by creating a routine of sorting it when you pick it up, discarding what you don't need and finding a home for what you do. Overtly visible clutter is a loud-and-clear message that something needs your attention. By ignoring it, you send yourself the message that you're not a priority.

## Desk/Office

Clutter in your home office could be suffocating your financial health. Perhaps you have unpaid bills you're avoiding, taxes you haven't filed, or bank statements that need reconciling. It might just be a dumping ground for mail. Whatever it is, devoting scheduled time to sorting clutter here is a surefire way to boost your bottom line.

The same goes for clutter in an external work office. While your work demands may result in a messy office, unnecessary clutter slows productivity and could act as a form of self-sabotage in your career. You may be overlooked for a promotion or find your job in jeopardy, again affecting your financial security.

A cluttered desk could also speak to a blocking belief about money. Do you judge those who have more than you? Do you fear others will resent you should your bank balance increase?

## Car

Clutter in the car is often the first sign of feeling overwhelmed. Are you frantically rushing from one thing to the next? Is your calendar too full? The clutter in your car could be your soul asking you for some downtime.

## Garage

Items in your garage quickly become part of the background scenery, so this area can almost always feel like a nonpriority. However, each time you leave or return home, the mess before you saps your energy. Even if you don't consciously see the boxes and bins anymore, your soul responds to them anew every day. Consequently, you operate from a disadvantage, never having enough energy to show up for yourself in the way you'd like.

## Attic

The attic, or *clutter's graveyard,* as I like to call it, can contain the most ties to the past, holding you back from moving forward. Maybe you're keeping heirlooms out of guilt, or your child's baby clothes in hope of clinging to those precious years. Much of what is in your attic is likely getting in the way of your advancing on your soul's journey.

## Body

Now here's something few people think of as clutter—the extra pounds you're carrying. However, this is the quintessential type of clutter that holds a deeper message. If shedding weight was just about eating healthy and exercising, we'd all be thin, but there's much more to it than that, and the messages this clutter has are powerful.

Excess weight is most commonly used as protection from others' energy, painful relationships, and nasty self-talk. You may use it to guard your vulnerability or sensitivity or to help you feel invisible. You might be stuffing down your emotions with food or trying to quiet your fears and insecurities.

Your spirit is calling out for love, acceptance, and compassion. Instead, we tend to beat ourselves up for being overweight. And what does that often lead to? More weight gain to soothe and comfort the sting of those messages.

## Relationships

Negative Nellies, chronic complainers, and perpetual pessimists: your relationships with these kinds of people are the ones that need to be cleaned up. Draining relationships often cause physical clutter to pile up as your spirit seeks protection from energy vampires.

Maybe you're holding a grudge or hanging on to anger over a past encounter. This is a toxic and far-reaching form of emotional clutter. It can tuck itself away in the recesses of your mind as it slowly chips away at your happiness. To tend to this type of clutter, I like to call on the tools of compassionate listening and forgiveness.

When I think about someone who has made me angry, to help facilitate reaching forgiveness, I try to remember that his or her behavior comes from a painful place. No one wakes up in the morning and thinks, "Who can I piss off today?" It's likely that something that's going on is making that person behave that way.

It can be incredibly difficult to forgive someone who you feel wronged you. And you shouldn't feel that by doing so you're saying what the person did is okay. Forgiveness, in fact, is more for yourself than anyone else. It's about setting yourself free from the situation and no longer ruminating about it so you can move on with your life.

You've likely heard the expression that holding a grudge is like drinking poison and waiting for the other person to die. To stop drinking the poison, I use a silly little mantra to get myself in check. I close my eyes, think of the person, and say, "She's not an asshole, she's just wounded." Sometimes I even sing it to myself to the tune of "He Ain't Heavy, He's My Brother." Whatever it takes to clear that clutter!

So whom do you need to forgive?

Sometimes the person you need to forgive is yourself. We are all doing the very best we can at any given moment, and when we know better, we do better. Use frustrating situations as learning opportunities. How can you do it differently next time? Be kind and gentle to yourself.

Loving yourself right where you're at is the fastest way to get where you want to be. No positive, long-standing change comes from a self-punitive place. You can't berate yourself to success, but you sure can love yourself there. Love yourself even with emotional and physical clutter. Doing so shows that your love is not conditional or that it only comes once the clutter has been cleared. When you practice compassion even with the current state of things, you'll be much more likely to make progress.

## A Worrying Mind

There's nothing that will clutter your mind faster than a ticker tape of negative thoughts and worry. Excessive worrying indicates a strong discomfort with feeling out of control. By obsessing over the what-ifs, you can fool yourself into believing you'll be prepared for whatever comes along; however, as the saying goes, "Worrying is like praying for what you don't want." By holding a loving space for your worried thoughts instead of letting them rule the roost, you teach yourself that *you* are your safe place, and over time, you'll notice it's easier to calm your mind and feel more centered.

Now, it's time to look at the specific clutter within these hot spots to clarify the message even further. You'll find these items have some things of their own to say.

## COMMON CLUTTER CULPRITS

As you dig in deeper, listen closely to the words that surface as you consider individual pieces or categories. You want to feel positive and supported instead of criticized or judged. That's the difference between an item that's clutter and one that's a treasured belonging.

If you don't love it, need it, or use it, it's clutter.

## Books

Books hold a lot of promise. Novels are a pleasant escape, self-improvement books offer advice on or answers to longtime struggles, and resource books are handy when you need a quick reference. If that was all they represented, choosing which ones to keep and which to get rid of would be easy.

But for many people, books can feel like dear friends. You may have gotten swept up in the stories and gone on adventures with the characters. How could you possibly part with them? It all depends on how they make you feel now. Just because you once loved something doesn't mean you should keep it forever. Keeping anything, including books, out of any kind of obligation takes up important energy in your life that could be available for something that is aligned with your current goals and values.

Books multiply quickly, particularly because they're easy purchases and can provide immediate gratification without even cracking the covers. Take a moment and think about your stash. How do you feel about how many you own? Are they well organized? Scattered in various rooms? Have you read most of them? Are the majority novels, self-improvement, or resource books? How does your body feel when you consider letting some of them go?

I took my client Roger through a quick exercise during one of our calls. While we were on the phone, I asked him to scan his bookshelves and pause on a title here and there, paying attention to any thoughts that came up. Most of his library consisted of unread self-improvement books.

As he paused to read a title, I asked if he felt guilty for not having read it, if he was excited about the help it might provide once he dove into it, and if he felt any tension or flutters in his body when he scanned the book.

Over and over he mentioned feeling a combination of excitement and guilt, including guilt over the excitement. He could remember buying a book with hopes of gaining insights and help, but then because he never read it, seeing the book made him feel, in his words, "guilty and pathetic."

We talked about his tendency to look for something or someone to rescue him because he felt stuck and hopeless and concluded that looking outside of himself for healing that could only come from within would leave him always searching.

Through our work together, Roger began to see his books as important tools on his journey—tools to access his own wisdom, instead of powerful pages containing the answers to all of life's mysteries. By convincing himself that the solutions to everything he struggled with were in those books, it was no wonder he wasn't reading them. The pressure that comes with the risk of having that kind of knowledge and still not being fulfilled or happy had been too much for him. Better to stay ignorant and have excuses for not making progress.

Now, not only was Roger able to sort his books more easily—he even donated several—he also became a passionate reader of those he kept and began making incredible strides toward the life he dreamed of living.

## Clothes

I'm sure you can guess the messages your clothes are sending you: you're not thin enough, attractive enough, stylish enough, fun enough, just . . . not enough. What hangs on that rod is more than just fabric, and it can make you feel pretty bad about yourself. The memories and feelings associated with those items can make cleaning out your bedroom closet much more difficult than it needs to be.

Some may trigger happy memories, others painful. Both can make it difficult to let go of them. Take thin or fat clothes as an example: "I'm going to save these jeans because I'm going to fit into them again someday," or "I've really done well with getting healthy, but I'm going to hang on to those clothes that are too big just in case I slip back." Either way, those clothes are sitting in your dresser or closet, taunting you like the books on your shelves, telling you that you're not good enough.

Go take a look in your closet or dresser. See if you can find five items you haven't worn for six months or more. Now ask yourself why you keep the piece of clothing. Is it a just-in-case item? Does it remind you of a happy time? Do you still love it?

Doing this is a great start in determining if your clothes truly represent who you are today or if they're interrupting your journey instead.

## Magazines

People love magazines! Like books, they can hold a lot of promises. Just picture the headlines you see at the grocery store checkout counter:

"LOSE 10 POUNDS IN 10 DAYS!"

"COOK LIKE A CHEF IN THREE EASY STEPS."

"THE ONE THING YOU NEED TO DO
TO FIND YOUR TRUE LOVE."

A stack of magazines drains your energy by being one more thing you need or want to read. They might also make you regret having spent the money buying them. And they might make you feel foolish for falling for the headlines.

My friend Kylie had stacks of magazines in her house, most of a particular publication she loved. She had already read them and enjoyed them, but she kept them in a box in case she wanted to go through them again. The problem? They'd been in that box for years.

She asked me if they'd be considered clutter even though she loved them. If you love something, it's usually not clutter, but the fact that they had been in a box for two years and she hadn't looked at them in that entire time changed that answer.

Because the magazines' articles addressed a lifestyle she dreamed of having, she feared that getting rid of them would mean recycling the dream too. I suggested she go through them and create a vision board (a collage of images and words on a poster board or paper) of her dream lifestyle to hang up somewhere she would regularly see it. That would be a much better tool for manifesting her vision than magazines stuffed in a box in the attic. She loved the idea, and by the next week she had her vision board hanging in her bedroom. And the remaining magazines? They went right into the recycling bin.

If you have magazines that are piling up for "someday reading," think about what that pile really represents. If it's nothing more than "I spent the money, so I should read them," into the recycling bin they go. And no, you don't have to go through them beforehand. If they've been sitting there for 3, 6, or 24 months, there's nothing in there that you can't live without. Keep this month's and last month's issues. But all the others? Gone.

Your resistance might say, "But I've got pages dog-eared that I want to refer to," or "What if I need that information?" When is the last time you referenced those pages? What do you believe you'll really be getting rid of if you recycle the magazines? What deeper purpose are they serving in your life? Close your eyes, take a few deep breaths, and inquire.

## Family Heirlooms

Family heirlooms often have a lot of expectations, obligations, memories, joy, sadness, and regret attached to them. Your grandmother's locket, family photo albums, your father's favorite recliner, your mother's formal dishes—items like these, when not cherished or wanted, can still be nearly impossible to pass on. Does getting rid of them mean you don't love your grandmother, mother, or father? Are you a bad daughter for no longer keeping something?

My father once bought me an adorable music box in the shape of a phonograph. I loved it because it came from him, and I loved the song it played. I remember the day he gave it to me. We were out poking around in some gift shops with my mom. When we got back in the car, he handed me the gift bag. I can still see the joy on his face when I opened it.

One day, it fell from a high shelf and broke beyond repair. I kept it, in pieces, on my desk for weeks because I didn't want to let it go. Then I realized seeing it broken made me sad. It no longer gave me the heartwarming memory of shopping with my dad and his giving it to me. All I thought about was that it was broken. So I got rid of it. While I miss the music box, by not having the obliterated remnants staring me in the face, I get to enjoy the memory of that day. Even now, after my dad has passed, I think about that music box and that day with love, even without the box being on my desk. The box broke, but my memory didn't.

I guarantee that Grandma is not looking down on you and thinking, "I'm so glad she still has that locket even though she doesn't like it." She's not in that locket. Only keep it if you cherish it. Whatever you decide, she'll be with you always.

If you don't love these items enough to use them or display them, they're clutter. If the items mean a lot to you, honor them. If they've been sitting in a box in your basement for the last five years, they can't mean that much to you. Reevaluate their worth to you and either say good-bye or make them a part of your life.

## Half-Done or Old Projects

I bet as you walk by the box of scrapbooking supplies or the half-painted canvas, your shoulders droop with disappointment over how long the project has sat undone. What messages are they sending you? "Oh, I really should finish that." "You'd never know I was excited to paint. I have all the supplies, but I've never picked up a brush." These items become tools to beat yourself up with for not completing that project.

Supplies or in-progress projects that have been ignored or neglected can validate negative beliefs you hold, such as "I don't have what it takes to see a project through to completion" or "I never finish what I start." But have you ever considered that maybe those items are no longer relevant to who you are now?

Dave Bruno tells a story in his book, *The 100 Thing Challenge: How I Got Rid of Almost Everything, Remade My Life, and Regained My Soul*, about the vast array of woodworking tools he acquired because he imagined himself as a "master woodworker." As he was paring down to just 100 items, he struggled to get rid of these tools. However, after he'd done it, he said he felt an incredible sense of relief. *Oh, good, I don't have to be a woodworker anymore*, he thought.

He hadn't realized how much those tools were telling him who he "should" be instead of who he truly was. So along with the tools, he let go of that false image of himself. And in doing so, he opened space in his life to focus on who he truly wanted to be—a minimalist sharing his vision with the world.

## Draining Relationships

Think about the people in your life—your tribe. Are they loving? Supportive? Inspiring? Do you often feel taken advantage of? Walked on? Are you exhausted after spending time with certain people?

Having relationships that drain you can send a message to yourself that you don't believe you're worthy of kindness or of being treated well or that your needs don't matter as much as everyone else's. It's this kind of thinking that keeps you in those relationships. Whatever you allow to happen will continue. Flip the script, and make your needs a priority.

Many of the tools and techniques you use to clear physical clutter can be applied to emotional clutter too. Emotional clutter is different from physical clutter in that it's about *feelings* rather than *stuff*. It's about what you're experiencing versus what you're seeing. Because it's intangible, it can be much easier to stuff away or avoid. The good news? You can change things up just by getting started on sorting and clearing—not just things, but your thinking too.

## *Action Time!*

What is your number one clutter hot spot?

What stops you from clearing it?

What is one step you could take to make some progress on opening that space?

Schedule a time and commit to taking that action!

Listen up! Keep an ear out for resistant and negative messages that come up, and jot them down. Giving them a voice quiets them more quickly than avoiding or ignoring them, and it saps them of their power. It also helps you see what's really behind the piles or drains.

.........................................................................

# Chapter 4

# Common Causes of Clutter

We've established that clutter is anything that gets in the way of living a life you love. Debt, grudges, stacks of books, overflowing dressers, your inner critic, excess weight, too many shoes or kitchen gadgets, unhealthy relationships, a draining job—the list goes on and on.

When you think of additional areas of clutter you may not have considered before, it can be a bit overwhelming. However, all clutter has common threads running through it. Instead of only organizing the stuff, if you deal with the threads, you'll be able to say good-bye to your clutter much more easily. In fact, you can stop it before it even becomes an issue.

Three common threads are:

1. Unrealistic expectations
2. Lack of boundaries
3. Old beliefs

Let's break them down one by one.

## UNREALISTIC EXPECTATIONS

The number one obstacle to clearing clutter is unrealistic expectations. You look at the piles and you can't imagine how you're ever going to do it all, so you freeze or tell yourself, *As soon as I have a block of time, I'll dig in.* I've heard countless clients say, "Once I have a free weekend, I'll clear out that garage."

Aside from the fact that you'll almost always find something more enticing to do than sorting clutter, the belief that you must have a huge chunk of time free before doing anything is just a deterrent.

Get this: you can feel the joy and elation of all your clutter being gone by just getting started. That's because success is in the action, not in the outcome. Pretty cool, eh?

**Success is in the action, not the outcome.**

Expecting yourself to tackle the entire closet at one time makes your inner critic throw a fit. It's too big for her, and it feels like a prison sentence. Break the project down into smaller chunks, and she'll get on board.

My favorite way to do that is by using the **Pomodoro Technique**. This simple time-management approach has you use a timer to break work down into manageable chunks. (The developer of the technique, Francesco Cirillo, used a tomato-shaped kitchen timer when he was in college. *Tomato* in Italian is *pomodoro*. Add that to your trivia toolbox!).[1]

This structure makes it easier to stay focused while helping you avoid the burnout that often comes with trying to do too much at once.

Here's all it takes:

1. Choose your task or project (going through books, drafting what you'll say when you set a boundary, getting caught up on your tax filing, etc.).

2. Remove all distractions. Shut down your e-mail, silence your phone, and close your door.

3. When you're ready to begin, set a timer for 25 minutes. Work consistently until the timer rings.

4. Take a five-minute break away from the task.

5. Repeat.

6. After four Pomodoro rounds (or Pom rounds, as I call them), take a longer break, like 20 or 30 minutes.

Using a structured approach to clearing clutter helps quiet your inner critic because you're baby-stepping along. She doesn't get as riled up that way. Sure, she may still resist the task, but the five-minute break at the end of the round provides a light at the end of the tunnel of sorts.

About that five-minute break: Keep in mind it's only five minutes, so plan accordingly. Don't expect to run to the grocery store or return a friend's call. Before you get started, come up with ideas for how to spend that time so you don't get into something that takes too long or too much brainpower. Something like:

- Standing up and stretching

- Getting a glass of water

- Stepping outside and taking a few deep breaths

- Throwing in a load of laundry

- Closing your eyes and giving yourself a little pep talk (*C'mon, Kerri, you got this. Let's do another round!*)

You may opt to have your Pom round be 20 minutes or 30 minutes long. It doesn't really matter. What does matter is that you keep the time frame realistic. No two-hour Pom rounds allowed!

When I first started using the technique, I doubted that I could focus on one thing for that long. It felt like an eternity. Then, as I got more comfortable with the idea, I began feeling like 25 minutes wasn't enough. I'd want to dive in quickly because I "only had 25 minutes." It was a pretty cool shift. Even my inner critic was vibing with this technique!

As you dig in, you'll learn the best approach for you. Pay attention to when you're tempted to throw in the towel. What's coming up for you in that moment? What's your inner voice saying? How can you address her rebellion? What does she need? Beware of those *shoulds*—"I should do it this way," or "I should work on it for this long." Remember, she's a clever one!

Be realistic about how long you'll work on your clutter. Trial and error will help you see how much bandwidth you have at any one time and discover the best time of day to have momentum.

As you begin to put action behind your intention, you will rally the support of that powerful Universal force that is waiting to be called upon, and soon you will find yourself in the flow, fast-forwarding to your dream life, even when you think it's out of reach.

My clients Debbie and Brett had gotten a bit bored living in London, where they owned a flat. They wanted to travel more, but they were mired down by everything it would take to make that happen. They felt overwhelmed by the logistics, the home repairs that would need to be completed to rent out their flat, what they would do with their furniture, self-doubt over whether they could actually make it happen, and more. Between their physical belongings and their overwhelmed thinking, they were drowning in clutter.

To get them started, we simply took their idea a little bit further. First, we brainstormed what they'd need to do to be location independent. They already had a virtual business that allowed them to work from anywhere.

"Just spout off what's whirling around in your head," I told them.

"We need to figure out if we want to sell our flat or rent it out. If we rent it, do we rent it furnished or unfurnished? If unfurnished, how will we sell our furniture? We'd have to pare down significantly to make ourselves more mobile. What would our friends and family think? We'd have to do some home improvements before selling or renting. Where would we travel? Can we afford to do this?"

And that was just the beginning. I'm sure you can relate to the barrage of thoughts that come up when you're considering "going for it," whatever that means to you.

Their first assignment was to spend one Pom round writing a list of the thoughts they shared and grouping them into categories: flat, business, fears, logistics, and so on.

Mind dumps and categorizing are great ways of handling mental clutter. Things always feel bigger in our heads because the brain is a computer, not a container, yet so often we use it as the latter. As a computer, it has limited storage space. Cram it full, and its processing speed will slow down dramatically. You can feel at peace instantly just by emptying your mind and freeing up your hard drive. Yes, instantly.

Learning to quiet your mind and clear mental and emotional clutter allows you greater access to your innate wisdom. Like Debbie and Brett, you already possess everything you need to be and do what you want. Life's noise just muffles and buries it, but intentional action and regular practice provide much easier access to it.

Debbie and Brett then spent one Pom round looking at the financial aspects of their idea, including renting versus selling the flat, a budget for the kind of travel they dreamed of, and the revenue from their business.

Once they sorted this out, they determined that it could really happen! As they went along, step-by-step, momentum picked up. As they concentrated on Pom rounds to check off the items on their list, some other tasks practically took care of themselves.

After deciding to rent the flat unfurnished, they had an auction house representative come take a look at their furniture. They had some pretty unique pieces and felt that would be the best way to sell them. The representative loved what he saw.

"I have a show coming up that these items would be perfect for," he said, "but I'd need to take the whole lot by the end of the month."

Debbie and Brett hadn't planned on selling the furniture so soon, but they took this as a sign from the universe that they were more ready than they thought, and off went their furniture. The only thing left behind was their bed, so for a couple of weeks they were sitting on beach chairs in their living room.

"We wouldn't have changed it for the world," Debbie said. "That nudge was just what we needed to fly the coop."

This is the power of putting action behind intention and not letting mental clutter stop you.

That's the power of the Pomodoro Technique: It gets you started. It gives you an attainable goal, and once you get the ball rolling, you get to experience the joy of success, which motivates you to keep going.

Realistic expectations keep your resistance in check and let you celebrate short-term goals to fuel your fire.

## BOUNDARIES

Boundaries are your best tool for clearing mental, emotional, and energetic clutter. Every relationship you're in requires boundaries, whether it's with your boss, family, friends, neighbors, co-workers, strangers at stores, spouses, or partners.

When you set boundaries, you teach people how to treat you. You let them know, whether through actions or words, what is okay and what isn't. These healthy and nurturing parameters help you build trust with yourself by letting in only what you truly want and what serves you best. You also send a clear message to the universe that you're willing to make yourself a priority.

When you don't set boundaries, your energy tank is almost always empty, and you have nothing left to put toward achieving your dreams and goals.

When clutter piles up, take it as a sign to think about where you're not taking the best care of yourself. Are you at everyone's beck and call? Is your calendar too jammed up with commitments?

How do you know if you even need a boundary? Consider the following questions:

- What am I tolerating in my life?
- Where do I feel taken advantage of?
- Whose phone calls do I dread receiving?
- What or whom would I rather not have to deal with?
- What am I saying yes to when I really want to say no?

A great way to start checking boundaries and your need for them is to pay attention to requests for your time, talent, energy, or company. Instead of automatically agreeing, pause and check in to see if you truly want to help.

If you feel compelled to say yes, ask yourself why. If it's anything other than a pure desire to show up and help that person, hang out with it for a bit.

You might say yes when you mean no if:

- You don't want to disappoint anyone.
- You don't want to risk not being liked.
- You believe that if people need you, they'll keep you in their lives.
- You'd feel selfish saying no.
- You were taught to put others before yourself.

While it can sound a bit clichéd, when you say no to others, you really do say yes to yourself.

The first step in setting boundaries is to become best friends with the word *no*. Even if you aren't an active participant in the local PTA, you're still a good parent. Even if you don't help your brother move, he'll still love you. Learning to sit with the discomfort that may come with disappointing people is crucial to your happiness.

Over the years, I've assigned several clients my Disappointing Challenge, where I ask them to disappoint at least one person each day for two weeks. Yeah, they usually gasp too.

This challenge helps you

- See how many requests come your way.
- Identify which requests drain your energy or frustrate you.
- Evaluate the relationships in your life.
- Reclaim your power and get back in charge of your time.
- Learn to say no firmly and graciously.

Without fail, each client who was willing to accept the challenge found it truly changed his or her life. One client said, "I was so nervous to take this on because I didn't want people to be mad at me, but I started with small situations like you suggested, and now I'm disappointing two and three people a day!" What she wrote next said it all: "I feel like I'm living life on my terms for the very first time."

If you face this emotional and energetic clutter head-on, I promise you'll be surprised by the results. No, it's not as difficult as you think. No, people will not freak out on you.

Yes, you will stand taller and have more confidence. And yes, you will be less afraid to put yourself out into the world.

Working on boundary clutter leads to cleaner relationships, less stress, and deeper connections with the people in your life. It also helps you identify which relationships you want to repair and which ones it might be time to say good-bye to.

It can feel scary to think about saying no. What if everyone stops contacting you and you end up alone? Who are you if you're not the favor doer?

**Feelings are to be felt, not fixed.**

Listen for the reasons you come up with to convince yourself to say yes when you don't want to. Chances are they're false stories you make up so you can avoid feeling uncomfortable about putting your needs first. The solution to that isn't self-sacrifice. It's showing yourself that you'll be fine even when you feel a bit shitty. After all, feelings are to be felt, not fixed.

In my work, I've found that the main reason people don't set boundaries is that they lack the language to do so. How can you make your needs clear without sounding rude? The rule of thumb when it comes to establishing these parameters is: short, sweet, and to the point. Once you start explaining your reasons for saying no, you invite the other person to challenge you.

Check out this ineffective boundary setting:

"My computer is acting funky. Could you look at it?"

"Oh, I can't. I'm going to dinner with a friend."

"It'll only take a minute. Could you do it after dinner? Or maybe tomorrow?"

"Hmmm, not sure. I'll have to see what my day looks like tomorrow."

"Okay, I'll call you then to see."

Now check this out:

"My computer is acting funky. Could you look at it?"

"Sorry, I don't have any time. I'd suggest calling your computer manufacturer's help line or doing some research. I'm sure others have had a similar issue. You can find lots of solutions online!"

See what I did there? I said no graciously, didn't give a specific reason for the person to debate, and offered a next step. It's clear, concise, and leaves very little room for pushiness.

Here's another example:

"I want to buy a new camera, and you're so good at Internet research. Next time you're online, could you see what the cheapest deal is for a Canon Rebel T3i?"

(Side note: Notice the ego stroking with "you're so good at . . ." This is a clever tactic that has worked on me numerous times!)

"I hear that's a pretty decent camera. I won't be looking for cameras anytime soon, but if I come across any deals, I'll let you know."

"See, I don't know anything about cameras like you do. I wouldn't even know where to begin to look."

"I'm sure you'll find something."

See how I left some doors open with "If I come across any deals" and "I'm sure you'll find something"? Both statements invite the person to keep me posted on their progress and to continue including me in their quest.

Now looky here:

"I want to buy a new camera, and you're so good at Internet research. Next time you're online, could you see what the cheapest deal is for a Canon Rebel T3i?"

"I hear that's a pretty decent one. I'm not in the market for a camera, so won't be doing any research on that soon. I suggest checking out Adorama or Amazon. Good luck!"

No open doors, and, again, suggestions for next steps that don't include me.

How about the dreaded dinner invitation from someone you'd rather not spend time with?

Ineffective boundary:

"Hey! I haven't seen you in ages. Let's grab dinner tomorrow night and catch up!"

"Oh, sorry, I can't tomorrow night. I've already got something on the books."

"This weekend, then."

"Oh, I've got a family gathering."

"Well, let's compare calendars then and find a day we both can do it."

And I'm trapped.

Until this approach:

"Hey! I haven't seen you in ages. Let's grab dinner tomorrow night and catch up!"

"Nice to see you too. I'm not sure when I'd be able to meet up. Hopefully my calendar loosens up someday! Take care."

Firm, final, and lighthearted.

Work requests can be tricky, particularly if you feel you'll jeopardize your position by setting a boundary. But it's possible even here.

Boss: "I'm going to need you to work a couple extra hours today."

You: "Unfortunately, I'm not able to work late today. With a bit more notice in the future, I'd be happy to stay and help."

This response shows you're a team player, but also communicates that you're not at the boss's disposal.

Watch for the voice that tells you you're selfish, a terrible person, or rude. Remember who that is: your inner critic, trying to get you to keep toeing the line.

If you decline a request to make cupcakes for the school's bake sale, you're still a good parent.

If you choose taking a bath over meeting someone for a drink, you're still a good friend.

When we're restructuring relationships, it often takes the other person time to adjust. Even if your boundary is clear and to the point, some people may push the envelope and keep asking. In this situation, simply restate your boundary until they hear you. Everyone eventually gets it.

"I know you said you can't make the cupcakes, but we have no one else. We really need you to help out here."

"I wish I could, but I'm not available."

"We'll have to postpone the bake sale if we don't have the cupcakes!"

"Geez, I wish I could help, but I can't."

Restating your position clearly, and as many times as necessary, without heading into over-explaining is foolproof. The good news is that when you practice setting boundaries with the people in your life, you'll eventually have less and less need to do so because you'll have taught them how you operate. Your energy will no longer invite excessive requests.

To get started, practice setting boundaries in low-risk relationships, such as one with a co-worker rather than a family member, or with a stranger at a store instead of your boss.

Let's say you're in line when a new register becomes available. The cashier says, "I can help the next person in line," and the person behind you goes in front of you. A low-risk boundary-setting practice would be to say in a friendly tone, "Excuse me, I'm actually the next person in line," as you make your way to the newly opened register.

Is it fun and comfortable? No. Is it a great way to exercise your boundary muscles? Yes. This is a chance to dip your toe into boundary setting. You don't know this person. You don't have a vested interest in maintaining a relationship with him or her. You're still being polite in your language, but you're standing up for yourself without the risk that goes along with it when it's a family member or close friend, and each time you set a boundary, it gets a little bit easier.

Many years ago, I worked with a woman who was the type who woke up talking. She was chipper, perky, and chatty right out of the gate. I'm someone who needs time to ramp up, so I dreaded walking into the office because I knew she'd come at me with the news of the morning and stories from her commute. I'd start getting annoyed on my drive in, which is no way to start the day. Then I slowly began resenting her. *Can't she tell I don't want to talk? Just let me shuffle to my office and wake up a bit, would ya?*

Then I remembered—she's not a mind reader. I needed to tell her to give me time to plug in to the day. It was time to let her in on the arrangement she was a part of.

"Hey, Linda, I'm not much of a morning person. Do me a favor and give me some time to settle in at my desk and wake up a bit before chatting. Thanks."

"Oh, okay," she said. "No problem!"

I immediately felt relieved by the idea of not gearing up for battle each day. Sure, Linda needed reminders, but it became a playful joke between us. She'd start talking to me right when I walked into the office, and I'd simply say, "Not awake yet, Linda," and that was enough to get her to pause and walk away. This boundary made for a much happier workplace and eliminated the mental clutter of dread, conversations with Linda in my head, and frustration over my space and time not being respected. Linda had had no idea she was doing any of that!

As I did with Linda, you'll likely have to remind people of your new boundaries. It's part of restructuring the relationship. There's going to be a learning curve for the other person no matter how much you want a permanent change immediately.

Once you've begun exercising your boundary muscles, you can start to tackle more significant relationships. Yup, I'm talking about those with family and close friends.

There are lots of ways to ease into boundary setting with higher-risk people. While a clear, direct conversation is great, it's not always needed. You can sometimes retrain people simply with your actions.

My client Sarah's sister bombarded her with texts and voice messages and would flip out if Sarah didn't get back to her right away. She was used to Sarah responding pretty quickly, and when she didn't, her sister would keep calling and texting. Sarah would finally respond, thinking there was an emergency, only to find out her sister just wanted to chat. To avoid conflict, Sarah started responding to her texts and messages right away and checking her phone frequently to make sure she didn't miss a call or text.

This was okay for a time, but then Sarah started to get fed up and resentful. When she'd see her sister's name on the phone, she'd roll her eyes. *Here she is again!* She was feeling robbed of her time by her sister's incessant messaging. But she wasn't being robbed. She was giving her time away.

It was time for some reconditioning. First, Sarah and I worked on establishing soft boundaries for her sister, like having Sarah wait 24 hours to return a call or text. Sarah would have to sit with the discomfort of knowing her sister was mad at her, but she knew she had to handle it; otherwise, they wouldn't have much of a relationship left.

Her sister naturally came back barking, "Why aren't you returning my calls?"

Knowing this was coming, we had crafted some language in advance: "I'm not always able to immediately respond to your calls or texts, so don't be surprised if there's a time gap before you hear from me."

In this case, Sarah's slowing down her response time and mentioning her inability to respond right away helped her sister get the message, albeit slowly. She first challenged the boundary by continuing to call and text at her regular frequency, but with Sarah not joining the dance, things slowed down. Her sister not only texted less and less frequently, but also began indicating why she was calling or texting so Sarah could gauge the urgency, if there was any. The messages now were more along the lines of "Just wondering if you're around to chat" or "I could really use your advice on something. Call when you have a moment."

While the transition wasn't smooth sailing for either of them, they quickly found that riding out the waves had been worth it. Their relationship grew closer, and they began being more honest with each other in every way.

Had Sarah's sister continued pushing back, a firmer boundary would have been needed. Something like: "You text and call me a lot. I don't have time to get back to you right away. I know you may not like that, but that's how it is. Trust that I will return your call when I can. No amount of additional texts or calls will make that happen any sooner."

Pretty clear, right? The good news is, rarely do conversations need to go there. As long as you put actions behind your boundaries, people will get the message. So don't tell your sister you can't get back to her right away but then get back to her right away. Don't say you won't be looking into deals on cameras anytime soon and then send the person some links.

Make sure your actions support your words. That's the key to having people respect and adhere to your boundaries.

Just as with any other clutter, consider how this type—draining relationships—might be serving you. There is a payoff to being a doormat, dumping ground, or over-giver—if there wasn't, you wouldn't allow it.

Why might you agree to dinner with that friend whom you'd rather not meet up with? Are you avoiding the discomfort of disappointing someone? Are you keeping your calendar full so you can tell yourself you're too busy to make the changes in your life that you've been talking about? Maybe occupying your time in this way protects you from taking some risks.

Similar to physical clutter, there are deeper reasons there. Investigate it as you did with the physical clutter, and find out what's really going on with those relationships.

Now let's look at the rules we impose upon ourselves by using outdated thinking.

## OLD BELIEFS

A belief is a rule we live by, but it's a rule we agreed to long ago and probably forgot about. It becomes a part of our being, and we don't pay attention to it anymore. Think of it as similar to the windshield on a car. It's there, but you don't notice it. You just look through it and go along on your way.

Beliefs act like filters in your brain, causing you to view the world in a specific way. Often, they skew the way you see things. They're created when you're very young, at a time when you're new to the planet and looking around, observing the primary people in your life to learn how to navigate the world. You're learning about what you should and shouldn't do.

Beliefs almost become our manual in life. That is, until we find out later that some (or most) of them aren't helpful at all. They were formed as survival tools for a child, not an adult.

You create these beliefs to find your spot in the world around you. At that age, significant parts of your brain have yet to develop, and you're egocentric. Think about kids— they think it's all about them. It's not because they're bad, but because that's the way their brains operate at that time. When children see someone behaving a particular way, they translate the person's action through the "me" filter: "How does that pertain to me?" "What does that mean for me?" "Oh, that's how I should do it/handle it/behave."

Let's imagine you saw your parents arguing, and they were screaming at each other and calling each other names. As a child, you would have translated the situation into instructions. "Oh, so when you're angry at someone, you should yell." Or maybe Mom stormed off and didn't talk to Dad for a couple of days, and you learned that when you're mad at someone, you shouldn't talk to them for a while.

The tricky thing with these "instructions" is that they morph into blocking beliefs that trip you up as you get older. Let's take the "not talking to someone when you're mad" example. Our child's mind learns not only how to argue, but also what the consequences are. That can easily morph into a belief like, "If I make someone mad, they'll leave me, so I'd better be agreeable and accommodating if I want to be loved." This belief turns you into someone who says yes to all requests and invitations despite a lack of desire, and what does that result in? Relationship clutter.

Because beliefs need constant validation, we gravitate toward people and experiences that prove our thinking right. Let's say you have an old belief that tells you your needs aren't important. Chances are you'll find yourself in relationships with takers, or you won't take good care of your health.

Beliefs are so powerful that even if you don't attract those who validate them, you'll actively seek them out. If you believe life isn't fair, you'll search for evidence of that. It's not that you are magically creating unfair situations by way of your thinking. Instead, your belief tells you life isn't fair, so to validate it, you're going to look to make that true. As Henry Ford said, "Whether you think you can or you think you can't, you're right."

While you usually create these beliefs for a good reason, such as feeling safe, making sense of your environment, or loving your family unconditionally, they can get in your way as an adult. By the time you're grown, you have a pretty fixed opinion of yourself. You think you're this and not that. You're not smart enough, attractive enough, worthy enough.

This cluttered way of thinking can prevent you from seeing all your options, trying new things, or believing you have what it takes. It can also manifest as physical clutter.

My client Sandy had three filing cabinets crammed with paperwork, and it was spilling into piles on her floor. She was drowning in printed articles and blog posts, magazine clippings, and pads filled with notes.

"I like to hang on to information I might need someday. If I don't know about something or need to answer a question, I can reference my files," she explained to me.

"When is the last time you referenced these papers?" I asked.

"Oh, I can't remember. It's just nice knowing they're there. Just in case."

"So they're like a safety net of sorts?"

"Yes."

As we dug deeper, I asked her what she'd be throwing away if she were to get rid of the files.

"Resources and references," Sandy said.

I reminded her that those things can easily be retrieved again, especially with the power of the Internet at her fingertips. "What would you really be throwing away?"

After a long pause, she said quietly, "It would be like throwing away my intelligence."

Now we were getting somewhere.

As someone who had always felt like the "dumb" one in her family, she believed all of her smarts were filed away in these drawers. Over time, as we worked on obliterating that old belief and replacing it with a strong, empowering one, Sandy began recycling papers like a champ. They began to feel like weights on her wings, and she wanted them gone.

She had thought she just had a storage or organizational issue and that she was too lazy to sort through the paperwork, when in fact the files had had a powerful purpose. They had been validating her old belief that she was not smart enough.

They weren't there to torment her. When they were looked at as a messenger, they helped Sandy see she had outgrown her limited thinking. In fact, when she got rid of the papers, she felt self-assured and confident!

Because beliefs are such an integral part of who we are, it can be tricky to identify them. A good way to start is to do an inventory of your past. Think back to what types of people surrounded you as a child. In what types of environments were you raised and taught? What was your neighborhood like? Who made up your circle of friends? What did you learn about how the world operates from their behavior, their experiences, and their words?

A journal is a great tool to use when doing this inventory. To prompt memories, you can write some short stories starting with things like, "When I was a kid and misbehaved, my father would _____" or "When I was in school, if I didn't complete an assignment, my teacher would say _____." You can fill in blanks such as, "When I succeeded at something, I was described as _____," or "When I didn't succeed, people said _____."

Play with the questions and fragments to come up with ones that relate to the area of your life where you're dealing with a lot of emotional clutter, self-sabotage, or blocks so you can begin to understand what your beliefs are and where they come from.

Another way to uncover your blocking beliefs is to listen for "if-then" statements. For example, if you say something like, "If I'm needy, then people won't like me," or "If I'm vulnerable, then I'll be a burden." That's a good indication of early programming that has turned into an unhelpful rule.

Also, listen for broad or generalizing statements that you use. Things like:

- "They're always out to get you."

- "Life isn't fair."

- "People are . . ."

- "You can never . . ."

- "Things never work out for me."

- "I always get the short end of the stick."

- "You can't have it all."

These statements act as emotional clutter that gets in the way of living your dream life. They're excuses, they're protection, they're scapegoats. By having blocking statements as part of your operating manual, you will continuously look to prove them right. If we didn't do that, we'd be going against our default operating system, making us feel a bit shaky, uncomfortable, maybe a little afraid, which would trigger that inner voice to tell you not to rock the boat. But if the beliefs you're operating from aren't helping you get where you want to go, it's time to flip the script.

When you get fed up with bumping up against a limiting belief and realize that you're sabotaging yourself, it's time to clear this emotional clutter. Your thinking is often the biggest clutter culprit, so let's do some work, shall we?

## Action Time!

This exercise is a three-part process to address the main reasons that clutter builds up.

**EXPECTATIONS:** Start by emptying your brain. Set a timer for 10 minutes, and in your journal, write down everything that's on your mind. It can be anything from "Take dog to the groomers," to "What to get Mom for her birthday," to "Clean out the linen closet." The idea is to empty your brain as completely as possible.

Next, review what you wrote and categorize the items under three headings:

- **Me:** things that only I can do
- **Someone else:** things that could be handled by another person
- **No one:** things that don't really need to be done at all

This will help you see what clutter you might be fabricating and what it is that truly warrants your attention.

Organizing your mental clutter begins the process of establishing realistic expectations. Instead of plowing full steam ahead with no plan in place, this gets you to evaluate what's truly important and what isn't. Doing so shows your resistance that you're going to be strategic and methodical as you implement change.

Finally, choose one item from the "Me" category and plan how and when you'll handle it. If it's a big item, be sure to break it down into small steps. Your resistance will let you know if it's too big!

**BOUNDARIES:** Review your schedule and commitments for the next seven days and evaluate how many of them support the bigger picture of what you want for your life. Note which items you could, theoretically, cancel.

Now it's your turn for the Disappointing Challenge! Yes, for the next two weeks, I want *you* to intentionally disappoint at least one person a day. I know that feels scary, but it's important to make that *No* muscle strong. If the idea of this freaks you out, start with easy letdowns, like waiting a bit longer to return a text or phone call or not participating in the office gift exchange.

To get the full benefit of the challenge, however, most of your disappointing needs to be a bit higher risk. Try declining dinner invitations from friends, letting your neighbor know you're not available to let his dog out, and changing your mind about a commitment you previously agreed to. Look for more ideas in your calendar.

This may sound like I'm asking you to be a bad friend, neighbor, or community member, and it might even feel that way, but that's the point. It will likely feel uncomfortable, but I want you to see that the fear you have about what will happen when you say no is unfounded. People will still love you, and you won't be forgotten.

Accepting this challenge is a testament to your willingness to tear down some old beliefs that have been getting in your way for years. This, combined with the belief-flipping exercise below, will empower you, quiet your inner critic, and desensitize you to the feared repercussions of saying no.

**BELIEFS:** This exercise will run the course of several weeks. It takes time to create and establish a new, empowering belief. Take it step-by-step as outlined below, and you'll be on your way!

1. *Identify the belief you'd like to reverse.* Consider any default thinking that gets in your way. Thoughts like:

   - I don't have what it takes.

   - I'm not motivated.

   - I have no willpower.

   - My needs don't matter.

   - I never finish what I start.

2. *Come up with a powerful opposite belief.* Using the examples above, opposite beliefs would be something like:

   - I have everything I need to succeed.

   - I easily break projects down into manageable steps and take action.

   - I'm patient and loving with myself as I step out of my comfort zone.

   - To be able to care for others, I must care for myself first.

   - I easily follow through on the projects and tasks that matter.

3. *Start keeping a Belief Book.* Once you have your new belief (one that makes you say, "Hell, yeah!"), write it down 10 times before bed every

night for at least two weeks. Keep your book on your nightstand with a pen as a reminder. You're about to have great access to your subconscious during your sleep, so it's a perfect time to plant this new positive seed.

4. *Act as if.* Now that you've been planting the seed for a bit, it's time to begin walking as if it's fully true and integrated. This behavior will be the validation the new belief needs to take hold. For example, you might challenge yourself to decline a handful of extraneous requests or invitations for two weeks to help validate your new belief that your needs should come first. Without action to back it up, your belief remains just an idea, and an idea has no power against a long-held limiting belief.

5. *Repeat as needed.* Whenever you find yourself defaulting to your old belief, revisit steps 1 through 4. It took years to lock your blocking belief in place, so be patient as you work to flip it. The good news is that it won't take as long to undo it!

By reversing the belief, you retrain your brain to look for hope and options instead of frustration and obstacles.

..................................................................................................

## Chapter 5

# Is Your Clutter a Handy Distraction?

Once you determine what the underlying threads in your clutter are, you still may struggle to get rid of it. Maybe you'd rather keep it? Your clutter might be helping you in ways you don't even realize.

When you consider it as a communication tool of your wise self, clearing clutter becomes an opportunity to graduate, spiritually, to the next soul level, and to begin living more fully and authentically. And that can feel scary. What will life look like then? Maybe it's better to keep things as they are rather than to risk change. It's the dreaded fear of the unknown. We hear that expression a lot, but is it even a thing?

Think about it. How can you fear something you don't know? It's impossible. The real fear is that you can't handle the unknown, and clutter is your protection. While your inner critic needs love, patience, and support, she also needs to know you'll be the one in charge of navigating this unknown. She needs you to show her it's your job to figure out the next steps and when you should ask for help. Only after you demonstrate your ability will she start to believe that you can handle whatever comes your way.

Let's say you're ready to publish your first blog post, but you're scared of what people will think (emotional clutter). What if they criticize your writing? What if they disagree with what you say? Worse yet, what if no one reads it? I mean, who do you think you are to even have a blog?

These fears are the voice of your inner critic, who is scaring you into not hitting PUBLISH. Remember, anything new is bad in her mind, and as the sensitive, vulnerable part of you, she is hesitant to put herself out there. What she's also doing, in her own way, is asking you how you'll take care of her should these scary things actually happen. Your inner critic is like a child. When they want or need something or are confused or frightened, kids sometimes beat around the bush and aren't the greatest at saying what they mean, so you have to infer what their concern is.

Your inner critic, no matter how tough she may seem, is not equipped to deal with negative feedback. Answering her questions yourself or getting support from a friend or coach shows her you're willing to do what it takes to strengthen your self-confidence and let go of what others think. She'll feel heard and taken care of, and as a result she'll be less likely to stand in your way as you go after your goals.

This is where small steps help you build trust with your inner critic. Maybe you could start by just jotting down some ideas for blog posts. Then you could create a draft of one. Then maybe you could edit the draft and find a good photo to go with it. As you take these steps, keep those lines of communication open with your critic. Check in with her. See how she's feeling. Don't leave her in the dust, or she'll come out kicking and screaming again. In my client Marjorie's case, she quieted her critic's temper tantrum with food.

Marjorie wanted to be in a loving relationship, but she didn't feel confident dating because she was heavier than she'd been in a long while. She was working on getting fit so she could feel better about her online dating profile picture.

For a couple of years, Marjorie had been seesawing when it came to her weight. She'd make great strides in losing weight for a few months and then slowly start eating sugary snacks again. She came to me frustrated about her struggle to get fit, hoping some accountability and clear action steps would help her stay the course. And for a bit, they did. That is, until I noticed Marjorie's tendency to eat more snacks the closer we got to uploading a profile picture and activating her online dating account.

As we explored more, she shared stories of how she'd never felt like she was good enough when she was growing up and how whenever she tried for something, she felt that she fell short. She also didn't have the most encouraging family. She felt rejected and alone much of the time.

"Could you be fearing that same kind of rejection from people on the online dating site?" I asked.

"Oh, sure," she said. "Wouldn't anyone? Dating is scary."

"I get that. But what if this fear of rejection is a reason you can't lose the weight? Because you won't activate your account until you have a profile pic you like, and you feel that can't happen until you're thinner, wouldn't it make sense to keep the weight on to help avoid that possible rejection?"

Long pause . . .

"Yup," she said quietly.

"Great! Then to help you feel more confident about yourself, let's work on the fear of rejection as an approach to helping you release the weight."

And so we did. It was a winding road to get there, but by learning to reject herself less, Marjorie no longer felt the need to wait until she was at a certain size to put herself out there. She activated her online account with a beautiful profile picture of herself, "full face and all" (her words), and started chatting with a couple of good guys the following week.

She'd believed the extra pounds she was hanging on to were saving her from rejection, but it was her thinking and history that were stopping her from putting herself out there. The pounds and the thinking? Both were clutter.

Marjorie may have told herself that once she lost weight, she would be happier or finally meet the love of her life. The idea of that happening is pretty exciting, and it can be fun to imagine how great everything will be. But with that excitement comes something else: doubt. What if, after achieving your goal, life isn't all you'd hoped it would be? What if you lose the weight but you still don't meet a romantic partner? What if you're as unhappy skinny as you were fat? Then what do you do?

You'd no longer have this basket to put all your eggs in. You'd have to face the fact that there's more to the equation than just a number on the scale. It can be tempting to hang on to clutter so you won't be disappointed and you'll have something to blame your unhappiness on.

It's fun to live in pursuit. We love the chase. It can be exciting to go after a goal. Think of the rush you get when you consider starting a diet on a Monday. You feel that buzz inside, excited to finally take some action. Then Monday comes, and you decide it'd be better to start next week, so you have doughnuts for lunch.

What if your desk is clear and you still can't get yourself to finish the book you're writing? What can you blame it on then?

**The pressure of the expectations is enough to keep the clutter on your desk, your dream partner at bay, and the pounds on your body.**

By keeping your desk messy, for example, you tell yourself you can't pay your bills because you have no space to do so. But by avoiding the bills, you're also making sure your bank account doesn't grow or your business isn't profitable. If you're sending out negative money energy, it's unlikely the universe will support you in getting any more.

"As soon as I organize my supplies, I'll be able to work on my art." "Once I get my wardrobe squared away, I'll look for a job." If anything about working on your art or finding a new job (or any other goal) feels scary or overwhelming, not dealing with the clutter is a great way to stall.

The old adage "Actions speak louder than words" is the main motto of that powerful energy that's waiting to rally behind you. You can say you want to improve your finances, but if you're blowing through money, not paying bills on time, or not using a streamlined bookkeeping system, your actions are saying just the opposite.

Debt is another big source of emotional clutter. If you dread the arrival of your bills, avoid looking at the credit card balances, or worry about how you'll make the next mortgage or rent payment, you'll be hard-pressed to increase your income.

The clutter you need to clear here is your behavior about your finances, so dig in deeper—what's the benefit to avoiding the bills? Maybe you don't have to face the fact that you spend more than you can afford to? Or maybe finances overwhelm you. Would you prefer to bury your head in the sand and subscribe to the "ignorance is bliss" mentality?

When you think about making more money, do you feel incapable of handling it? Do you have any negative thoughts related to wealth or the wealthy? Are you worried about being judged? Do you criticize those who have more money than you? Do you believe it's not spiritual to have financial abundance?

Your clutter could also be acting as that boundary you're too nervous to set or don't even realize you need. When you don't let people know your needs or you allow them to treat you in a disrespectful way, your frustration or substitute protection can show up as clutter.

My client Monica recently bought a place in the countryside, and everyone was asking her when the housewarming party would be. The idea totally stressed her out. But instead of being honest about it, she extended the unpacking process so she had an easy answer.

"Oh, I'm still settling in."

The boxes and bags became the boundary she wouldn't set. While it was somewhat effective in the short term, it meant living in a cluttered home, and it prevented her from enjoying the beauty of her new space. Instead of tidying up her home when company was coming over, she'd clutter it up to support her story that she was still settling in!

Together, we crafted language that would set a loving, firm boundary, letting her friends and family know the real deal.

I suggested she respond with something like, "I've decided not to throw a housewarming party and will be inviting people over from time to time instead."

"That sounds kind and clear," Monica said. "I would feel comfortable saying that."

"Great, then you won't have to worry about fielding this question over and over again from the same people."

"But what if they push? Like by telling me all the reasons I should have a party?"

"That's the beauty of the boundary, Monica," I said. "You simply restate your position. A simple, 'I understand what you're saying, but I've decided not to have one.' And you can say that over and over again until they get it. It will feel uncomfortable, but that discomfort will slowly shift from you to them as they witness you holding your stance."

I challenged her to set her boundary the very next time anyone brought up a party, and to e-mail me and let me know she had. When I got her note, I was thrilled for her! She wrote, "No one even gave me a hard time! Well, one person was a little persistent, but after my second time stating my case, even she stopped. I can't believe something so simple could be so impactful!"

In theory it's simple, but the stories we tell ourselves make boundary setting so much more difficult. When you come up with a way to say it that is firm but kind, it's not so scary.

Another common clutter-as-boundary tactic is cramming your calendar with commitments, obligations, and appointments. If you don't have an open space in your book, you can't say yes to invitations you don't have the courage to decline. You let your calendar do it for you.

When my client Jennifer retired, she was excited to have lots of free time on her hands. Little did she know, her son was psyched too, because then she'd be available to babysit whenever he needed her to—or so he thought.

The first couple of times he asked, Jennifer happily agreed. She loved spending time with her grandchildren. Then the requests kept coming. Could she pick them up from school, take them to soccer, and feed them dinner? Jennifer was torn. She felt she should help her son and enjoy quality time with her grandchildren, but she struggled with feeling frustrated, taken advantage of, and exhausted. It wiped her out to run around with the kids.

Saying no to her son never entered her mind as an option, so instead she made herself unavailable by volunteering with various local groups, joining a regular exercise class, and working at the hospital welcome desk. This way, when her son asked her to babysit, she could legitimately say she was busy. The problem was, she was still wiped out by the end of the day and annoyed by how filled her time was. Even though she was scheduling things she liked, her reason behind doing it was weighing on her, so she couldn't enjoy the activities.

Together, we came up with a compromise. She'd agree to watch her grandchildren one day a week, and her son could choose which day helped him the most. When we found a way to say it in a way she felt comfortable with, she agreed to take on the challenge of telling him. Because setting boundaries with family can be a particularly sensitive subject, we arranged to speak right before and right after her conversation with him. It's easy to feel shaky when you're exercising new muscles, and sometimes you need someone to hold you up.

Once again, the story she'd been telling herself didn't match her son's story at all. He'd thought he was doing her a favor by giving her so many opportunities to spend time with his kids. When she explained to him that it was just too much for her and that she'd be happy to do the one day a week, he fully understood and agreed.

See, that's the other thing with clutter. We pile on the stories in our minds, making it bigger, heavier, and more intimidating than it needs to be. Check out your story, and you'll almost always be pleasantly surprised.

Clutter is a virtually bottomless source of information. And all this time you thought it was just an annoyance!

## *ActionTime!*

To help determine how you might be benefiting from hanging on to your clutter, complete the following sentences. Jot down the first thing that comes to your mind. Don't censor it. This is for your eyes only. Then reread your answers and dig even deeper.

Once my clutter is gone, I'll be able to _____.

I'm excited about being able to finally do that because

_____.

I'm nervous about being able to finally do that because

_____.

I'll be happier once I'm finally able to do that because

_____.

The consequences I'll have to face once I'm finally able to do that are _____.

......................................................................

*Chapter 6*

# Let's Get Practical

Although you've begun to look at your clutter in a whole new way and understand the role it's playing in your life, the fact remains: you've got too much stuff. What do you do with it while you're discovering the message in the mess so you can get some sanity *now*? Let's explore some processes and approaches to help you pare down what you have and limit what you bring into your life in the future.

Clutter can become part of the scenery after a while. As you look around to identify not-so-obvious clutter, try to look at your home and work environments with fresh eyes. And you don't have to do it alone. Evaluating and sorting can be much easier (and more fun!) when you have the right kind of support.

My client Lucy loves to hang on to things. Lucy's daughter, on the other hand, loves to get rid of things. Her daughter was the perfect person to help Lucy say good-bye to some items she'd been holding on to for years. They have the kind of relationship where Lucy's daughter can lovingly nudge Lucy to get rid of a little bit more than she would on her own, and Lucy feels heard and respected when she firmly states that she wants to keep something.

Be careful not to ask someone who you know will criticize you, shame you, or judge you. You want the help of someone who will be able to empathize with and hold a safe space for you.

Only you can know if you'll do better on your own or with someone else helping you. My mother has no problem getting rid of clothes, but she has strong emotional connections to certain household items, such as Christmas decorations. While she's okay parting with some, she'd rather have someone else in the family take them instead of giving them away. Her clutter clearing is much more successful when one of her kids is there to help her come up with ideas of others who can enjoy the decorations, even if they're not in the family.

Another thing she struggles with is recycling greeting cards. It's helpful for her to talk through any guilt she might feel in getting rid of them. She likely wouldn't clear out these items on her own, but with the right kind of support, she can honor her personal process.

My mother-in-law finds sorting household items easy but struggles with items that came from her deceased father or that are otherwise sentimental. When she and I go through items together, she has a chance to share her feelings, thoughts, and stories, which, like my mom, makes it easier for her to decide what she wants to keep versus what she's ready to let go of.

As you read through the approaches to clearing and dealing with common clutter culprits, remember that you're not alone. Asking for help and support is a beautiful way to care for your sweet, vulnerable self.

Reflect for a minute about the amount of each type of clutter you have and how it came into your life. What was the underlying motivation for first acquiring an item?

- Do you use retail therapy as a way to cope with life's challenges? What if you were to practice feeling the difficult emotions instead?

- Do you find it difficult to pass up a sale, even if it's on an item you don't want or need? Do you suffer from IMNTS syndrome (I Might Need This Someday)?

- Do you have difficulty declining a hand-me-down from a friend or family member? Where else in your life do you struggle to say no?

- Do you accept heirlooms from family members out of guilt?

- Does grabbing anything that's being given away fill a void in you?

- Do you feel loved if someone offers you something and worry that by declining, it will mean you're rejecting their love?

Buying or acquiring something new can give us a fix or a boost when we're feeling low. However, when that thing becomes part of your clutter, it does you more harm than good. Instead, consider how you can give yourself what you need rather than making a purchase.

Your first line of defense with clutter management is to limit the items you bring into your life by being selective in what you accept and buy. Let's explore a couple of examples to see how you can do that.

*Decline hand-me-downs.* Unless it's an item you've wanted for a while or know you'll get a lot of use out of, politely decline your friend's/sister's/boss's offer of that shirt/ necklace/statue. It can be tempting to accept it, because who doesn't like free stuff? Also, you'll likely fear hurting the person's feelings. But just as with any other boundary opportunity, decline briefly and graciously: "Thanks for thinking of me, but I'll pass. I'm sure someone is going to love it!"

*Cut unwanted items off at the pass.* The main times when you'll likely find yourself the recipient of unwanted items is during the holidays and on your birthday. If there are things you want, don't be shy about telling someone. If they ask what you want for Christmas, it's tempting to politely say, "Oh, nothing, thank you," but if they asked, chances are that you'll be getting something, so it might as well be something you want. Offer up a few ideas within a reasonable price range.

Blowing off the question can be rude, so it's better to respond. If you truly don't want anything, consider suggesting a charitable donation instead. "There's really nothing I need or want right now, but if you'd like to make a donation to <insert favorite charity here> in my honor, that would be nice."

*Buy quality over quantity.* When you're in the market for a new outfit, couch, or computer, consider shopping at stores whose products are of high quality. We've become such a disposable society that it's easy to build up an inventory of 10 pairs of jeans and 30 pairs of shoes.

Several decades ago, a piece of furniture was an investment that would stand the test of time and could even be passed down to future generations. Today, people are swapping out their furniture every couple of years. As a result, our landfills are overflowing, and it's easy to forget the global cost of buying more cheaply made products.

The same goes for clothing. According to the documentary *The True Cost*, 80 billion pieces of clothing are purchased worldwide every year, up 400 percent from 20 years ago.

Most of these clothes end up in landfills (85 percent of textiles are sent there, even though 95 percent of them can be reused or recycled[1]).

Consider the idea of a capsule wardrobe, which is where you have a handful of essential, classic, high-quality pieces that won't go out of style that you can mix with seasonal favorites, or a small collection of favorites that change with the season. This removes not only a lot of physical clutter, but also mental clutter. The decision of what to wear is much easier when you have less to choose from!

*Sort your mail.* The best way to get a leg up on what comes into your house is to sort your mail as soon as you get it. Which piece is junk and which is important? Put the junk mail right into the recycling bin. To make it easy, put the bin somewhere that's convenient to access, perhaps at the side of your house or in your kitchen.

Once you've identified the mail that's worthy of coming into your home, do your best to continue to sort it once it's inside. Open envelopes and recycle any extraneous papers, such as advertisements that come with bills or extra envelopes. Keep only those things that you need to follow up on and do something with.

Speaking of bills, it's helpful to have a filing system set up to show the universe that you are a good steward of your wealth. As the bills come in, either in the mail or electronically, file them accordingly. Before I went paperless, I would put my bills in a letter organizer on my desk in order of due date. In the same spot, I also had return address labels, stamps, and my checkbook.

I now schedule a bill-paying date on my calendar each month and go through my electronic folder of statements, paying them in one fell swoop. You can just as easily schedule two or more dates on your calendar monthly if your bills are due at different times of the month.

**Tip:** You can change the due date of credit card bills to a time of the month that works best for your income. All it takes is a quick phone call or a change to your online account.

To limit the amount of mail you receive, consider opting out of some common junk. You can get your name taken off catalog lists by calling the toll-free number on them and asking to have yourself removed from the mailing list. Or to filter even more of your mail, check out the Data & Marketing website at https://dmachoice.thedma.org.

You can also opt out of prescreened credit card offers by visiting www.optoutprescreen.com or calling 888-5-OPT-OUT (888-567-8688).

Still getting phone books? Me too, until I visited Yellowpagesoptout.com to opt out.

Like snail mail, e-mail can accumulate quickly. To support your commitment to simplify your life, take a moment to unsubscribe from e-mail lists so you don't have to spend time deleting them every time they come. While it doesn't take a lot to delete unwanted e-mail, it does take an energetic toll each time those messages come in. This is another opportunity to practice handling the source of clutter instead of constantly putting out fires. A great resource for unsubscribing to many e-mail lists at once is Unroll.me. By signing up for a free account, you can see a list of everything you're subscribed to at a compatible address and quickly unsubscribe in one fell swoop!

For those e-mails that you keep, consider creating a folder system in your e-mail program. One client of mine uses a process that I think is brilliant. She created the following folders within her inbox and manually files her messages accordingly:

**Action:** e-mails that you must follow up on, reply to, or do something with

**Waiting:** e-mails where you have done your part and are waiting to hear back from someone

**Someday:** newsletters and other e-mails that are not timely and can be read at your leisure

**Archive:** stuff that's handled and done but still needs to be kept

You can also set up rules or filters that will make your e-mail program automatically put incoming messages in appropriate folders. For example, I have an e-mail address reserved for sale and promotional e-mails. I created a folder for that e-mail address and set a rule in my program to automatically put any e-mails sent to that address in the folder. This way, I don't have unimportant e-mails clogging up my primary inbox, where it's easy for the important ones to get lost in the shuffle.

## PARING DOWN WHAT YOU ALREADY HAVE

As you work on downsizing, remember to keep those expectations realistic. Instead of cleaning and organizing your whole office, start with the left side of your desk. When working on clothes, begin with half of the hanging clothes in your bedroom closet. With books, look over two shelves on your bookcase.

Come up with small steps that will help you get started. You'll likely continue beyond the small step, but even if you don't, you'll be further along than you would've been if you'd planned to do the entire closet and then done none of it.

When fear or resistance come up, we default to A-to-Z thinking. You're here, and you want to be there. Trying to speed from start to finish is the quickest way to set yourself up to fail. If you want to cross the chasm, you've got to build a bridge. The fastest and most sustainable way to get to the finish line is by taking consistent, small steps. Use the Pomodoro Technique. If you need help remembering to keep your expectations in check, stick a note on your computer that says, "Pom round," or set a reminder on your phone that reads, "What's my very next step?" or "One small step at a time."

## Clothes

Statistically, we wear 20 percent of our wardrobe 80 percent of the time,[2] so make it a habit to review your wardrobe at the end of each season. What items did you wear the most? Use this information as a clue about the types of clothes you love. Are these favorites still in good condition? If not, are they repairable, or is it time to replace them with similar items?

Which items did you not wear at all throughout the entire season? These are the ones to let go of, unless, of course, they're items for particular occasions. However, you should still evaluate how much you like it and if it fits well before deciding that it should stay.

If there is something you didn't wear that doesn't have a particular purpose yet you struggle with letting it go, take a few moments to ask yourself what motivates you to keep it. Listen for the message underneath.

Maybe your college T-shirts remind you of a time when you felt limitless, eager, excited, and as if anything was possible. Struggling to get rid of the shirts is more about your desire to feel that way again and less about wanting to wear those shirts. You might think that if you let go of those T-shirts, you'll be letting go of that part of you, those memories, and those experiences.

To help clear the clutter, challenge that thinking. How did you feel in those glory days? What is it about that time that brought you such joy?

Now, consider your life today and how you could bring that same feeling back. Sure, it's not going to look the same—you won't be heading off to frat parties or playing college soccer again—but it is absolutely possible to get that feeling in a way that is aligned with who you are today.

Clearing the clutter from this subconscious place invites you to address the thoughts and feelings first, which then makes it much easier to clear and maintain a clean, open space.

When you look at your skinny jeans, they may remind you of a time when you were at or close to your ideal weight, but they may also remind you of a time when you and your friends would go out and paint the town red, pre-kids and -mortgage, taking spontaneous weekend trips away. Those great memories will be with you even when the jeans are gone. And getting back into those jeans won't make your current responsibilities disappear, but whether those jeans fit or not, they can be a sign that it's time to schedule a monthly girls' night out. The question is, How can you have the same fulfillment in your life that those jeans represent?

Some clothes might remind you of times you'd rather forget. Hanging on to these items makes it nearly impossible for better times to come along, particularly in the area of your life that the item represents.

Let's say you still have your ex-boyfriend's sweatshirt or the comforter from when you lived together. The old energy wrapped up in these items may be taking the space in your life where a new relationship would be. It's as if your relationship seat is fully occupied. If you're looking for love and striking out, take an inventory of your stuff to see if you're hanging on to anything from a past relationship—something that makes you mad, sad, or regretful.

My client Mark purchased a custom-tailored tuxedo for a fund-raiser he attended with his longtime girlfriend, the coordinator of a nonprofit organization. Unfortunately for Mark, it wasn't only funds that were raised that night: allegations that his girlfriend was messing around with a co-worker were also raised—by the co-worker's wife.

Ever the gentleman, Mark saw the event to the end and waited until they got home to ask his girlfriend about the rumor. As her shoulders sank and her eyes dropped to the floor, he had his answer.

Even a year after breaking up with her, he still felt sick to his stomach every time he looked at the tuxedo. It reminded him of her betrayal and lies.

Part of our coaching work together focused on Mark's desire to get married and have a family. He had been dating, but nothing was working out. Naturally, he was gun-shy and found it difficult to trust. Although he had been working on moving past the painful situation, he felt blocked.

"Have you ever thought about getting rid of that tuxedo?" I asked Mark.

"No," he said. "I paid a lot of money for it, and it fits like a glove."

"Have you worn it to other occasions since the fund-raiser?"

"No. I've had a couple other opportunities to, but it pisses me off to look at it."

"So, it fits like a glove physically, but energetically it's suffocating you. What if having that tuxedo hanging in your closet is botching any possibility of meeting Ms. Right?"

Mark was skeptical that one thing could have anything to do with the other, so we took a baby step and had him store the tuxedo away so it wasn't in his face every day when he got dressed.

After he did, he began to realize that he had been tensing up before opening his closet doors and now breathed a sigh of relief when he didn't see the tuxedo hanging there. He also had a couple of promising dates once he put the tuxedo in storage. Maybe it had been affecting him more than he'd realized.

"It's crazy to think an inanimate object could prevent me from meeting someone great," he said.

"It's not the tuxedo that's keeping her away. It's what it means to you. The tuxedo is a physical representation of your pain and your ex-girlfriend's betrayal. No matter how brilliantly it fits your body, it no longer fits your soul."

I encouraged Mark to keep his eyes and ears open for opportunities to pass the tuxedo along. Perhaps he could consign it or donate it to a charity.

The very next week, he learned that his company had teamed up with a local school to coordinate formal-wear donations for underprivileged kids going to the prom. This was a cause Mark felt particularly close to because he hadn't been able to afford a tuxedo for his prom. And there it was: validation from the universe that it was time to pass the tuxedo along. Thanks, Uni!

Mark's skepticism was now out the window, and he was eager to get rid of more draining clutter. Five months after donating his tuxedo, he met the woman who is now his fiancée, and he was happier than he'd been in a long time.

That charity drive was going to happen whether or not Mark was thinking about getting rid of his tuxedo. But because he was focused on finding a new home for it, he noticed the information about the charity drive. On any other day, he might have missed that announcement entirely because it wasn't on his radar.

You know when you learn a new word and you suddenly see it everywhere? Same thing. That word was always going to be on that sign or in that book. Your new knowledge of it didn't suddenly make it appear there. The difference is that you noticed the word because your focus was attuned to it after your having just learned it. This is how opportunity works. It's always nearby waiting for you to accept it, but with clutter in your life, it's hard to see.

Think about what it is you say you want more of in your life. If that were to show up, would you be energetically available, open, and clear enough to even see it? If your awareness is cluttered up, your lens can't be focused to see the gifts because you're looking through a dirty filter.

## Books

Books can hold a lot of energy, promises, solutions, rescues, or escapes. There's a lot going on in those pages, and that can make it tough to say good-bye. The best way to get started is to dive in without a lot of thought. Doing rapid-fire sorting in the first round connects you to your gut, which always has your best interests at heart.

Give this a go:

1.  Gather as many books as feasible in one room.

2.  Do a quick, gut-reaction sort into piles of Keep, Donate, and Maybe books. Don't labor over decisions here. You are practicing listening to your intuition as you do this part of the sorting process.

3. Take the Donate pile, box up or bag the books, and put it by the door so you can take it to your car the next time you go out.

   At this point, you'll have already experienced the thrill of success. You've created the space in your life that is necessary to recognize what the universe has to offer. You've taken action that supports your desire for a richer and fuller life. And the universe will respond, so pay attention to any coincidences that pop up.

   Maybe you were just thinking about your sister, and she calls. Maybe you've been considering taking a self-defense class and a flyer for one comes in the mail, or perhaps you've decided to let go of something and an opportunity to pass it along appears.

4. Go through your Keep pile. Does each and every book there truly deserve a place in your life? Because the physical and energetic space you have in your life is finite, anything and everything must be worthy of occupying that space. If you're on the fence about any books in this pile, move them to Maybe.

5. Now it's time to dig into the Maybe pile. The books in this pile can be very telling about how you treat yourself, the ways in which you sabotage your success, and what blocking beliefs you're operating from.

   What prompted you to put each of these books in this pile? Is one a gift you would feel guilty getting rid of even though you don't have a desire to read it? Is one an expensive textbook from college that it would feel wasteful not to keep? Maybe one is a self-help book that resonated with you, but you're frustrated that you still struggle with that aspect of your life and you've kept it with the idea of reading it again and actually doing the exercises this time. One might be a book you wanted to read when you bought it, but you haven't yet and are not sure you will.

If you can't easily move a book from the Maybe pile to the Keep or Donate pile, spend some time investigating why. Open your journal and write this question at the top: "How does this book make me feel?" Then let it flow. Freewrite without any censoring, editing, or judging. Let that inner voice speak. It's the source of your wisdom, your wise self, your heart.

Put your writing aside for a bit (at least an hour or two, but ideally overnight), then read what you wrote from an observer's perspective. What does this book represent? What promises does it hold? What strings are tying you to it? Dig deep here. Move beyond the guilt over the money you spent on it, beyond your sadness over the difference it didn't make in your life, beyond the regret over not practicing what the author suggested. If the book makes you feel worse about yourself more than it makes you feel excited or inspired, it's time to say good-bye to it.

If the book (or any other item among your clutter) was a gift, I can assure you that the person who gave it to you wouldn't want you keeping it out of guilt. Guilt is not what they wrapped in that package for you!

Now that you're ready to get rid of books, here are some suggestions for finding new homes for them:

- **Coffee shops or cafés.** While I wouldn't bring more than three or so, many coffee shops have bookshelves for sharing.

- **Little Free Library.** More and more of these little house-shaped boxes are popping up in towns all over the world. Neighbors are building them or purchasing them to install in town, where anyone and everyone can take or leave a book. Check out LittleFreeLibrary.org to learn about the history of the nonprofit that runs it and for information on how to get one in your neighborhood.

- **Used bookstores.** Yes, these still exist, and they are always looking for more donations. Some will even give you credit toward the purchase of new books, but just be sure you only purchase books you love!

- **Prison Book Program.** One of the few effective methods of decreasing the recidivism rate of incarcerated individuals is education. Check out their information online at prisonbookprogram. org/resources/other-books-to-prisoners-programs to find a list of programs that supply books to inmates.

- **Goodwill Industries International.** Goodwill is a great organization that uses the money made from the sale of your donations to fund job training and other services.

- **Local thrift stores.** Donating to small, local thrift stores ensures that you'll directly impact the people in your community. Whether it's because the items are offered at affordable prices or the revenue made from sales is circled back into community services, it's quite rewarding to support these little shops.

## Magazines

Magazines, especially if you have numerous subscriptions, can pile up fast. If you don't read a certain magazine anymore, cancel your subscription. In the meantime, you don't need to flip through or read a magazine that's been sitting around before getting rid of it. You can put it right into your recycling bin or check with your local library, fitness center, doctor's office, or nursing home to see if they'd like some issues.

If you find it difficult to get rid of any magazines, dig into your resistance like you did with the book exercise. What might be going on? A friend of mine has issues of *Coastal Living* magazine from years ago. She does display them on a shelf like her books. However, her attachment to the magazines is more about her love of all things nautical and the many great memories she has of summers spent at the beach and on her family's boat than about the content of those magazines.

Should she choose to recycle the magazines, she won't be recycling her memories with them. Those will be with her always. Although I haven't convinced her to get rid of them yet, I give her a pass because she truly loves them, and if you love something and treat it with respect (as she does by displaying them), then it's not clutter!

## Sentimental Items

Your relationships with sentimental items can change over time. Just because you cherished something at one time doesn't mean you will forever. If you're past your love for the item, it's time to say good-bye. If the item makes you smile when you see it, then it's not clutter. However, if it goes back in a box after you smile, I'd encourage you to dig deeper. What's stopping you from displaying the item or keeping it somewhere you'll see it often? Sure, we all have mementos that we don't put out. I challenge you to limit those items to one small box.

Maybe you used to collect figurines, but you don't feel passionate about them anymore. If you don't feel ready to donate the entire collection, consider keeping one as a reminder of that time in your life and donating the rest.

Bottom line: When you keep things out of guilt, you're keeping much more than just that item. You're keeping a whole lot of energetic and emotional baggage with it.

## Kids' Artwork

If you can't bring yourself to throw out your children's artwork, there's a cool service that will archive it for you. Artkiveapp .com supplies a prepaid shipping label to make it easy for you to send the artwork to them to scan into your private Artkive account. Then, you can choose to order a hardcover book of the prints, or choose a favorite image and they'll print it on a beach towel, tablet cover, shower curtain, puzzle, and more. Pretty cool, eh?

## Greeting Cards

Greeting cards are another big item that people keep out of guilt. Just like gifts, the sender's intention wasn't to pack guilt into the envelope. He or she simply wanted to send along their wishes. It's okay to read the card and send it right to recycling.

If there's a personal note that really moves you, take a picture of it or cut it out. The same with the cover of the card—if you love it, save it. One of my clients made a beautiful collage with the notes and covers she kept. Any time she's feeling down about herself, she refers to the collage and gets an immediate boost.

## Photographs

Believe it or not, your initial photograph sorting will go very quickly. Here's how to begin:

1. Gather all your pictures in one place.

2. Go through and get rid of any extraneous paper, envelopes, or negatives that you no longer need or want.

3. Using the Pomodoro Technique, go through the pictures and put aside any that are not good enough, meaning they are blurry, damaged, unattractive, etc.

4. Go through the rest and eliminate those that are of people you'd rather not look at or places or events you'd be happy to forget about.

5. Go through what's left and make a pile of those photographs that you absolutely adore or

want to give to others. Find ways to display the photographs you love and chose to keep so you can enjoy them every day.

## Unpacked Boxes

Do you still have unpacked boxes from when you moved three years ago? Chances are you don't need or want what's in there. After all, you haven't used anything in them or even looked in them in years! Take one quick look through the boxes if you feel you must, but then let them go.

If it's hard for you, dig into the why. Maybe you are someone who suffers from I Might Need This Someday syndrome. If so, you're certainly not alone, but if you haven't needed the contents of the box for a year or more, it seems like you can live without it just fine.

There are, of course, exceptions to this rule. You may have not used your car's spare tire in more than a year, but that's not something you want to get rid of, obviously. So naturally, use your judgment here, but be careful not to give yourself too much slack.

If you're tempted to keep something because you might need it someday, ask yourself, "Why do I really want to keep this?" Pay attention to the first answer that pops up.

As you downsize your belongings, do your best to avoid renting a Dumpster. The landfills don't need your help filling up! Besides, there are lots of creative ways you can get rid of items.

Maybe you know someone who could use or might want them. After the major downsizing of our belongings in preparation for selling our house, I invited my niece to shop in my basement before we took the items to the thrift store. She was moving into her first apartment and needed just about everything.

She scored artwork for her walls, drinking glasses, silverware, a coffee table, an end table, a living room chair, and more. The idea that these items were going to a family member who was so grateful to have them made getting rid of them even easier.

Check out the Clutter-Clearing Resource List at the end of the book for more ideas on where to send your stuff. Some of these approaches take more time and effort than just throwing something away, but in addition to treating our planet kindly, knowing that someone else *will* enjoy your items is almost infectious. My wife often jokes that I'd get rid of anything that's not nailed down, and at times, she's right because it's so fun to give things away!

When you dive into these practical action steps of sorting, clearing, and creating systems, be gentle with yourself. Under-promise and over-deliver. That's the best way to keep your inner critic in the game. Commit to doing at least one Pomodoro round to get started. Then, if you feel like you're in the zone and motivated, keep going. Remember, baby steps are key.

I work with clients all the time who have bursts of motivation that enable them to make some progress on organizing their spaces and their minds, but then they hit a wall. They can't seem to finish the job, and wonder why.

As a coach, I tell them that this is where the magic happens. It's at this roadblock that we can find out what's really going on with their clutter. There's a reason they can't get the clearing done, or that the stuff comes back again and again.

If you find yourself up against a similar wall, use it as an opportunity to step back, check in, and see what's really going on.

## Action Time!

Ready to dive in? Get ready to feel the powerful effects of small steps! Let's take three examples from the previously mentioned common clutter culprits and begin chipping away at them. To start implementing the processes and ideas mentioned in this chapter, dive into the steps below.

## MAIL

Starting today, work on developing a system for handling your mail effectively:

1.  Begin your sorting as soon as you go to the mailbox, separating the "keep" items from the "trash."

2.  Put recycling into the bin immediately.

3.  Destroy or shred any mail containing sensitive information, such as financial details, addresses, phone numbers, or credit card offers.

4.  Designate an area in your home for the rest of the mail that needs your attention (bills, correspondence, etc.).

5.  Determine when and how you will handle those items. Daily? Weekly? To help make this a routine, establishing consistency is key.

Now, after having completed the steps above, write down any resistance or pouting your inner critic is chattering about. Dig into those thoughts and brainstorm how you might address them. Look for the real reason underneath them, and don't fall for the surface message.

## BOOKS

Commit to doing at least one 25-minute Pom round on a book sort:

1. Take one shelfful (or a section of one) or stack of books and do a quick sort into three piles: Keep, Maybe, and Donate.
2. Now go through the Maybe pile and sort those into Keep or Donate.
3. Go back through the Keep pile to be sure those books still deserve spots on your shelf.
4. Pack up all the Donate books in bags or boxes.
5. Determine where to donate the books.

Acknowledge any resistance, thoughts, fears, feelings, or messages that come up so your inner critic feels heard.

## WARDROBE

Commit to doing at least one 25-minute Pom round in your bedroom closet or dresser drawers.

1. Choose a small section, such as one shelf, two drawers, or half of the closet.

2. Start with a quick sort, like you did with the books. Can you find five items to easily put in a donate pile?

3. Review your clothes from the previous season. Is there anything you didn't wear even once? Perhaps it's time for it to go.

4. Bag up all donations and identify where you'll be dropping them off. (See Clutter-Clearing Resource List.)

5. Look at your calendar and pick a day this week to make the drop-off.

Once again, have a notebook or voice recorder handy to capture any thoughts or feelings that surface as you work. We always want your inner critic or resistance to feel like part of the process, at least at the beginning, until she learns to trust you to fully take the reins.

She'll likely try to talk you out of your decluttering, telling you it's a fruitless waste of time. Don't believe her! She just needs your encouragement and reassurance that all is well.

# Chapter 7

# Turn Your Clutter into Cash!

So you've investigated, you've begun to understand the message in your clutter, and you've sorted. Now you're ready to make some money!

When we decided to sell our fully furnished, 2,000-square-foot house, we knew all the contents weren't coming with us. We also knew we could make some good money if we were willing to put forth a little effort. And it's a good thing we were willing to; otherwise, we wouldn't have stumbled upon the buyer of our house on Facebook!

After identifying what we were keeping, we spent a couple of Pom rounds taking pictures of and measuring the furniture and other big items we planned to sell. To avoid being overwhelmed, we didn't worry about anything else at this point. Remember, realistic expectations!

Melissa, being the Virgo that she is, created a spreadsheet listing each item and our asking price. She also noted where we listed it and when. If you have many items you're trying to sell, this is a great way to keep track of them. When the items sold, she added the sale prices to the spreadsheet, which motivated us because we could easily see how much we'd made thus far.

Here's a sampling of our bigger sale items:

- Outdoor wicker furniture set: $350

- Dining room set: $500

- Queen-size guest bed: $100

- Hardwood flooring (200 sq ft): $350

- Concrete pavers (300 pieces): $250

- Washing machine and dryer: $700

After all was said and done, we made more than $5,000! Not too shabby, eh?

Whether you choose to sell online, host a yard sale, or donate for a tax deduction, all options can leave you with a fatter wallet. To get you started, here are some tips and tactics for getting the most bang for your buck.

- **Craigslist.org.** By now, most people have heard of Craigslist, a portal for a variety of purposes—job searching, apartment hunting, car shopping, and some other "opportunities" that shall not be mentioned. One of the main reasons people use Craigslist is to buy and sell items. With clear categories and anonymized e-mail addresses to contact sellers at, it makes finding items and buyers and interacting with them clean and easy.

  When you offer to sell something on Craigslist, prepare to haggle. Prices on this site are considered negotiable unless the ad indicates "firm," so set your amount accordingly.

Once you've found a buyer and agreed on an amount, it's time to determine how to make the exchange. For safety reasons, Melissa and I never met anyone alone, and whenever possible, we met in a public place like a shopping plaza parking lot. Many police stations now offer their lobbies or parking lots as safe meeting spots for online sellers and buyers.

If the item was too big to transport and the buyer had to come to our house, we made sure not to be home alone and to let someone else know a person was coming over to buy something. Better to be safe than sorry!

Before getting started, I suggest creating a free Craigslist account so you can have a handy inventory of all your listings, allowing you to easily repost items that have gotten buried under other sellers' ads.

- **Facebook online yard sale groups.** On Facebook, search for groups in your area by typing your town's name and then "yard sale," or something along those lines. They're everywhere! Look for groups with a lot of members, and once your membership has been approved by an administrator, be sure to read the group rules. I don't like to waste my time on poorly run groups that are filled with advertisements. The rules posted by the administrator will give you a sense of how clean and streamlined things are. Also, be sure to follow the rules so your posts aren't deleted.

Facebook caught on quickly that members were using groups in this way and redesigned them to look more like Craigslist by including fields such as location, cost, and condition. The platform has also made it easy to post in multiple groups at once.

Once you and a buyer connect, follow the same precautionary steps and measures as for selling on Craigslist. This transaction is a great opportunity to practice boundary setting! In your ad or post, include something like, "Must pick up in (your chosen location here)" or "Can meet in the grocery store parking lot in the evenings."

- **Amazon Seller Central.** Amazon is a great option if you're interested in selling to a larger audience. Create an account and you'll be on your way!

  If you're selling a non-unique item (meaning anything that's not one of a kind), you can search Amazon for the product and simply click on the small button in the right margin that says, "Sell on Amazon." That will fill in all the necessary details and even use the same picture found online. So easy! You'll also see what others are selling the item for so you can beat the lowest price.

  I've sold several unopened collectible LEGO sets this way and made a pretty penny. While the percentage of the sale price that Amazon takes can be a bit hefty—it varies by category, but is 15 percent for Toys & Games, plus a small closing fee—it's well worth it for the ease of listing and managing the sale, the large reach of the website, and the time it saves on buyer communications.

You can choose to ship the items yourself as they sell (note that it almost always costs more to ship than Amazon charges the buyer), or you can send your items to Amazon in advance and have them take care of the fulfillment for a fee.

- **Consignment shops.** Clothes, furniture, musical instruments, antiques—there are consignment shops for all sorts of items. Each store has its own policies and processes. Stop by and inquire about what the store consigns, its regulations on item condition, the length of time your items will be on the floor, what happens if they don't sell in a certain amount of time, and what percentage the shop takes.

  I used a local shop for clothes that were in great condition but I no longer loved or wanted. My store took 40 percent and kept the items on the floor for 90 days, after which unsold pieces were donated. I could have arranged to go back and get anything that didn't sell, but my motto is "Once it's out of my house, it doesn't come back in."

  While that percentage may seem high, it's relatively standard for clothing consignment shops to take 30 percent or 40 percent. Because the process was so easy for me, it was well worth it. After spending 10 minutes setting up an account at the shop, whenever I dropped off more clothes, I simply included a note with my name and e-mail address in each bag and then waited for my inventory list and, later, my checks to arrive. As an added bonus, I was supporting a local business.

- **Decluttr.com.** Through this site, you can sell CDs, DVDs, games, electronics, and books. You either enter the numbers in or scan, using their app on your smartphone, the bar code on your item or search for the type of electronic device that you're selling, answer a couple of quick questions, and get an instant offer.

   Once you have at least $5 worth of products entered, Decluttr will send you a PDF, including a free shipping label. Pack up your items, attach the label, and send the box off. Upon receipt of your box and verification of the included products, you'll be paid the next day by check or direct deposit.

   We used this service for CDs and had a great experience.

- **Traditional yard/garage/tag sales.** Sure, these can be a lot of work. Okay, who am I kidding? These *are* a lot of work. The prep, the pricing, the organizing, the displaying, the advertising, the selling. But they can also be kind of cool. I realize I might be in the minority, but I like to meet members of my community that I might not have otherwise and walk around, working the crowd, answering questions, and making sales. I find it fun! At least for a couple of hours.

   When planning a yard sale, resist the temptation to sell small, inexpensive items, such as kitchen utensils and knickknacks. Save your energy for the big sellers—furniture, toys, curtains, candles, sports equipment, and gardening tools. Glassware and books are a dime a dozen (sometimes literally). You'll find it more rewarding to donate these items.

Set yourself up for success by being completely prepared the night before. Your ads may say the event starts at 8 A.M., but there are always early birds who show up 30 to 60 minutes before that. It's tempting to leave things like pricing until the morning, but you'll regret it. Grab some pricing stickers from the office supply section of your local drugstore or dollar store and, even as tired as you are, take the time to price everything before bed. Doing so means an extra hour of sleep the next morning!

I've held several yard sales and found the best marketing tools to be Craigslist (they have a garage sale category) and bright poster boards hung on telephone poles around town. For your Craigslist ad, post it no earlier than the Friday before; otherwise, it'll quickly get buried under the other listings. Also, be sure to advertise it in Facebook sale groups.

I asked most of my customers at my last yard sale how they'd learned about it, and 65 percent came due to signs hanging in the neighborhood. The other 35 percent came from Facebook and Craigslist, with the majority from Facebook. No need to spend money on newspaper ads anymore!

Have your coffee or tea ready in the morning, and sell, sell, sell. Nothing that leaves your house should go back in, so at the end of your sale, put the remaining items in your car and head off to your previously identified donation center.

- **Personal website.** If you have a lot to sell, like we did, consider putting together a simple website with pictures and prices of everything. This is something we did (and by *we*, I mean Melissa). We then directed everyone to that site, where they found all the goodies and information they needed. There are several basic, free, do-it-yourself site-creation services that you can use, such as Weebly.com and Wix.com. They're user-friendly, so don't be intimidated if you've never created a site before. No coding necessary!

If selling is not your thing, you may be able to make money indirectly using the itemized tax deduction for charitable donations. Find a local thrift store or donation center and make some deliveries. Not only will you feel great helping out others in need, you'll also save some dough. Just be sure to get receipts for your records.

## *Action Time!*

- Find a Facebook yard sale group near you and poke around a bit to get the lay of the land. To begin your search, visit www.facebook.com/ groups. When you find one, ask to join.
- Create a Craigslist account to easily keep track of all your listings. Review the types of items that are available for sale to get ideas.
- Identify five items to sell, and post them in your new Facebook group or on Craigslist.

## Chapter 8

# The Gifts of Your Newly Created Space

You made it! You've just taken a huge step toward getting a handle on the clutter that has been blocking your progress. You've created space to welcome in more money, deeper relationships, a more fulfilling career, better health, and a whole lot more. With the channels now open, prepare to see some real magic happen.

Keep your eye out for synchronicities and unexpected gifts. Maybe your car repair bill will be less than you anticipated or your child will unexpectedly hug you and tell you how much he or she loves you. These are evidence of the beautiful force that now has the space to swoop in and support you.

> When you clear away what you no longer love or need, you make space for unlimited gifts and abundance to come your way.

You'll find that with this reclaimed space and energy, life just seems easier. Your clarity will be sharper, your motivation will increase, and you'll feel lighter and happier overall. Yes, clutter clearing is that powerful!

It's so powerful that doing this work in an intentional way benefits the whole world! Getting rid of anything that's not adding to your life frees you up to add greater value to the lives of your family and friends, your community, your country, and so on. And by eliminating physical clutter responsibly (by donating, selling, gifting, or recycling) instead of adding to overflowing landfills, you're playing an important role in minimizing your community's clutter.

Imagine the energetic shift in a town that no longer needs to house a huge pile of trash and junk because people are repurposing, recycling, and sharing items instead of throwing them out. The air will be cleaner, energy will flow more easily, citizens will be happier, climate change will begin to slow, butterflies will land on your shoulder, and money will fall from the sky.

Okay, I might be taking it a bit too far, but you get the picture. Because all of life is one big energetic conversation, helping that energy flow more freely will naturally result in better connections and relationships for you and those you encounter.

Remember the key to staying in the flow: taking consistent action, one small step at a time. Make a move, then watch for the universe's response. Then take another step, and so on. Stay on this path, and soon the obstacles that tripped you up before will become little pebbles you'll easily kick out of your way.

When you feel stuck, reach for the tools you learned here. Because you've not only cleared clutter but also excavated the messages within it, you now have a leg up on your clutter.

Even without having fully integrated your learning yet, you're already on to clutter's game. You're willing to listen to what it's trying to tell you, so get in the habit of asking, "What's stopping me from taking action?"

Keep your expectations realistic and your steps manageable. Yes, challenge yourself to do a bit more than you think you can, but be careful not to set the bar so high that your resistance shows up kicking and screaming. Your inner critic is still learning to trust you, so it's critical that you break down steps way more than you think you need to. Doing so will also give you the space and time to be present and stay connected to the message in the mess.

Use the Pomodoro Technique. Despite knowing how effective it is, I often forget to practice it, so I have a note near my computer that says "Pom" to help me remember. I stick that note in the middle of the screen if I know I'll need it the next day. Sometimes I also set a reminder titled "Pom" or "Small Steps" on my phone. Set yourself up for success!

Let this guide be a living and breathing support system that you can tap in to over and over. Go through this book more than once. Do the exercises slowly and intentionally. You'll be at a different place each time you do, and you'll learn more and more about yourself and your patterns with each pass.

Finally, as you clear your clutter, consider thanking it for the lessons it provides and the opportunities it gives you to trust yourself more and more.

"Really, Kerri? Thank my clutter?"

Yes, as ridiculous as it sounds, sending it on its loving way allows you to hang on to the power you've reclaimed from it.

"Thank you, Clutter, for helping me see where my life needs some love and attention."

And thank you, dear reader, for taking this journey with me.

# Clutter-Clearing Resource List

## POMODORO TECHNIQUE
**www.pomodorotechnique.com**

This powerful time-management tool will help you put parameters around your clearing and make significant progress easily.

## FREECYCLE
**www.freecycle.org**

This is a nonprofit organization made up of more than 5,000 groups around the world, each run by local volunteers, where neighbors get and give items freely in a concerted effort to keep things out of landfills. You can search for your local group on the organization's website.

## CRAIGSLIST
**www.craigslist.org**

Craigslist offers lists worldwide. You can post in the "free" category or sell items here.

## GOODWILL INDUSTRIES INTERNATIONAL, INC.
**www.goodwill.org**

This nonprofit accepts household items, including clothes.

## AMAZON SELLER CENTRAL
**sellercentral.amazon.com**

## FACEBOOK ONLINE YARD SALE GROUPS
**www.facebook.com/groups**

Search for one near you.

## ANIMAL SHELTERS

Animal rescue shelters are always in need of blankets and towels, even if they're not in the best shape. Find your local shelter to pass on these leftovers.

## SECONDARY MATERIALS AND RECYCLED TEXTILES
**www.smartasn.org**

To sustainably get rid of ripped or stained clothing, rugs, or any other textiles that are unusable in their current form, check this site to see if there is a donation bin in your area. Textiles can also be brought to your local H&M clothing stores.

## BETTER WORLD BOOKS
**www.betterworldbooks.com**

This is a great resource for ideas for book donations, including where to locate their drop boxes.

## HOUSEHOLD ITEMS
**www.habitat.org/restores**

If you're remodeling, there's no need to rent an expensive Dumpster! Donate things like kitchen cabinets, toilets, hardwood floors, doors, windows, building materials, and furniture to Habitat for Humanity's ReStore.

## CDS AND DVDS, INCLUDING CASES
**www.cdrecyclingcenter.org**

You'll find lots of great info at CD Recycling Center of America, and they make it easy for you to recycle these items, plus inkjet cartridges, printer cables, and more!

**Decluttr.com**

Through this site, you can sell CDs, DVDs, games, electronics, and books.

## MAIL

To remove your name from catalog lists, call the toll-free number on the catalog and ask them to delete you from their mailing list. Alternately, you can visit http://dmachoice .thedma.org to decrease the amount of junk mail you receive. Don't let the catalogs pile up and have this be another to-do!

For mail addressed to "Resident," you need to call the individual mailer to be removed.

To opt out of prescreened credit card and insurance offers, visit www.optoutprescreen.com. You can choose to opt out for five years or permanently. You can also call 888-5-OPT OUT (888-567-8688).

For phone books, visit www.yellowpagesoptout.com, enter your name and mailing address, and select which directories you want. Or change "all" to "none" to stop them from coming altogether.

## E-MAIL
**Unroll.me**

Easily unsubscribe from several e-mail lists at once.

## PAPERWORK/BILLS/STATEMENTS
**www.suzeorman.com/resource-center/record-keeping**

Guidance is provided on how long to keep financial documents.

## EMOTIONAL CLUTTER
**www.thetappingsolution.com**

For support with trauma or emotional clutter, explore the Emotional Freedom Technique (tapping).

# Endnotes

## Chapter 1

1.  Self Storage Association. "2015–16 Self Storage Industry Fact Sheet." July 1, 2015. www.selfstorage.org/LinkClick.aspx?fileticket=fJYAow6_ AU0%3D&portalid=0.

2.  MacVean, Mary. "For Many People, Gathering Possessions Is Just the Stuff of Life." *Los Angeles Times*. March 21, 2014. articles.latimes. com/2014/mar/21/health/la-he-keeping-stuff-20140322.

## Chapter 4

1.  Pomodoro Technique. https://en.wikipedia.org/wiki/Pomodoro_ Technique.

## Chapter 6

1.  Stoeffel, Kat. "You Only Wear 20% of Your Wardrobe Regularly." *New York Magazine*. April 18, 2013. http://nymag.com/thecut/2013/04/you-only-wear-20-percent-of-your-wardrobe.html.

2.  Ibid.

# Acknowledgments

A heartfelt thank-you goes out to my big sister, Cheryl, whose support, sympathetic ear, and guidance during the writing of this, my first book, and throughout the years have helped me show up in ways I often thought unlikely to happen. Thanks, sis.

Thank you to my mom and dad for their unwavering encouragement and excitement and for the solid, loving foundation they provided that allows me to do the work I do and be the woman I am.

Thank you to my father-in-law, Bill, and mother-in-law, Jeanenne, for their love, support, and humor that reminds me to lighten up every now and then.

Thank you to my family, Steven, Janice, Donna, Tom, Lisa, Walter, Michelle, Mark, Riv, Karen, Ryan, and Brendan, for the unique and special relationship I have with each of you. I am blessed to know you are always in my corner.

Thank you to all my nieces and nephews, who help keep me young at heart and hopeful for the future.

Thank you to my dear friend and editor extraordinaire, Lisa Foulke, for her expert eye and honest feedback.

Thank you to Hay House Publishing for their faith in me and their support in sharing this work with the world.

Thank you to my editor, Lisa Cheng, for her insights, suggestions, and easy and effortless style.

Finally, my undying devotion and gratitude to the love of my life, my wife, Melissa, without whom I truly could not have written this book. She is my biggest cheerleader, my best audience and sounding board, and the most patient woman I know. Thank you for loving me in good times and bad. We really do make the best team.

# About the Author

**Kerri Richardson** is a lifestyle designer and coach with more than 15 years of experience. She has worked with thousands of people throughout her career, challenging them to play bigger, shatter expectations, and pursue their unique adventures. She lives in Boston, MA, with her wife, Melissa, and their two fur babies, Kiva and Kaya. You can visit her online at kerririchardson.com.

# Hay House Titles of Related Interest

*YOU CAN HEAL YOUR LIFE, the movie,*
starring Louise Hay & Friends
(available as a 1-DVD program, an expanded 2-DVD set, and an
online streaming video)
Learn more at www.hayhouse.com/louise-movie

*THE SHIFT, the movie,*
starring Dr. Wayne W. Dyer
(available as a 1-DVD program, an expanded 2-DVD set, and an
online streaming video)
Learn more at www.hayhouse.com/the-shift-movie

***

*ESTATE SALES MADE EASY: A Practical Guide to Success from
Start to Finish,* by Victoria Gray

*THE TAPPING SOLUTION: A Revolutionary System for Stress-Free
Living,* by Nick Ortner

All of the above are available at your local bookstore
or may be ordered by contacting Hay House (see next page).

***

We hope you enjoyed this Hay House book. If you'd like to receive our online catalog featuring additional information on Hay House books and products, or if you'd like to find out more about the Hay Foundation, please contact:

Hay House, Inc., P.O. Box 5100, Carlsbad, CA 92018-5100
(760) 431-7695 or (800) 654-5126
(760) 431-6948 (fax) or (800) 650-5115 (fax)
www.hayhouse.com® • www.hayfoundation.org

\* \* \*

**Published and distributed in Australia by:** Hay House Australia Pty. Ltd., 18/36 Ralph St., Alexandria NSW 2015 • *Phone:* 612-9669-4299 *Fax:* 612-9669-4144 • www.hayhouse.com.au

**Published and distributed in the United Kingdom by:** Hay House UK, Ltd., Astley House, 33 Notting Hill Gate, London W11 3JQ *Phone:* 44-20-3675-2450 • *Fax:* 44-20-3675-2451 • www.hayhouse.co.uk

**Published and distributed in the Republic of South Africa by:** Hay House SA (Pty), Ltd., P.O. Box 990, Witkoppen 2068 info@hayhouse.co.za • www.hayhouse.co.za

**Published in India by:** Hay House Publishers India, Muskaan Complex, Plot No. 3, B-2, Vasant Kunj, New Delhi 110 070 • *Phone:* 91-11-4176-1620 *Fax:* 91-11-4176-1630 • www.hayhouse.co.in

**Distributed in Canada by:** Raincoast Books, 2440 Viking Way, Richmond, B.C. V6V 1N2 • *Phone:* 1-800-663-5714 *Fax:* 1-800-565-3770 • www.raincoast.com

\* \* \*

## Access New Knowledge.
## Anytime. Anywhere.

Learn and evolve at your own pace
with the world's leading experts.

www.hayhouseU.com